SCARECROW AREA BIBLIOGRAPHIES
Edited by Jon Woronoff

1. *Middle East,* by Sanford R. Silverburg. 1992.
2. *Eastern Europe,* by Rebecca Gates-Coon. 1993.
3. *U.S. Foreign Relations with the Middle East and North Africa,* by Sanford R. Silverburg and Bernard Reich. 1994.
4. *South Asia,* by David N. Nelson. 1994.
5. *Bibliography of the Soviet Union, Its Predecessors, and Successors,* by Bradley L. Schaffner. 1995.
6. *Asian States' Relations with the Middle East and North Africa: A Bibliography, 1950–1993,* by Sanford R. Silverburg and Bernard Reich. 1994.
7. *East and Northeast Africa: A Bibliography,* by Hector Blackhurst. 1996.
8. *Caribbean,* by Marian Goslinga, 1996.
9. *Western Europe Since 1945: A Bibliography,* by Joan F. Higbee. 1996.

Western Europe Since 1945: A Bibliography

Joan F. Higbee

Scarecrow Area Bibliographies, No. 9

The Scarecrow Press, Inc.
Lanham, Md., & London
1996

SCARECROW PRESS, INC.

Published in the United States of America
by Scarecrow Press, Inc.
4720 Boston Way
Lanham, Maryland 20706

4 Pleydell Gardens, Folkestone
Kent CT20 2DN, England

British Cataloguing-in-Publication Information Available

Library of Congress Cataloging-in-Publication Data
Higbee, Joan Florence.
    Western Europe since 1945 : a bibliography / by Joan F. Higbee.
       p.   cm. — (Scarecrow area bibliographies ; 9)
    Includes index.
    1. Europe, Western—History—Bibliography. I. Title II. Series
Z2000.H52 1996 [D840] 016.9—dc20 95–48831 CIP

ISBN 0–8108–3112–0

Contents

Editor's Foreword

Since 1945 Western Europe has undergone half-a-century of change. Change has occurred in virtually every field: art, culture, economics, politics, science, and technology. With the emergence of the organizations that culminated in the European Union, far-reaching integration has affected the authority of the state and created a whole new hierarchy. Indeed, even while the Europeans themselves changed, the population base has changed with immigration from other regions. The differences between the Europe of 1945 and 1995 are dramatic.

This fact enhances the value of a bibliography of Western Europe since 1945. Among the numerous books, some describe the status quo at different times as well as at present, and others attempt to explain the process of change. Many of the works cover Western Europe as a whole, focusing on specific subjects or sectors. Others deal with the situation in the various countries, again structured according to subject and sector. A final section includes titles on significant persons who brought about the change. This structure makes it easier to locate books on the persons, places, events, and topics a reader may be seeking.

It was a challenging task to bring together these many strands, one to which the author devoted much time and effort. Joan F. Higbee is a rare book librarian at the Library of Congress in Washington, D.C. She has long had a special interest in Western Europe, having received a doctorate in Romance Languages, then written the *Scholar's Guide for Southwest European Studies,* and also serving as chairperson for the Western Europe specialists section of the Association of College and Research Libraries, American Library Association. *Western Europe Since 1945: A Bibliography* is a further contribution to our knowledge of that central, and still changing, region.

Jon Woronoff
Series Editor

Introduction

From the ashes of World War II emerged an historic struggle to form a union of European states through the peaceful abolition of national frontiers. In 1958, the Treaty of Rome officially created the European Economic Community. In 1987, the Single European Act amended that treaty to promote creation of a unified Internal Market. Western Europe since 1945 has progressed from individual nations concerned with colonial relationships and war to states involved in constructing and maintaining supranational European institutions. When, in November of 1994, Sweden voted to join the European Union, it offered the possibility of integrated states reaching from the Arctic to the Mediterranean, from Ireland to the Baltic Sea. Yet as the movement toward federation increases so do efforts to preserve the cultural identities of individual nations. And while the Maastricht Treaty provides for a common foreign and security policy, individual states confront, in the face of growing nationalism, the pull of internal multicultural forces.

Western Europe Since 1945 is a bibliography of books in the humanities and social sciences that have been written predominately in English and that collectively reflect transformations in the culture of European nations following World War II. They depict evolving relationships between increasingly interdependent states. Works written before World War II are included when they instigated or foreshadowed change, captured the vision of a world soon to disappear, or represented a significant work in the life of an author important in the years after 1945. Although many works cited have been published in the last ten years, earlier imprints have also been included in order to provide analysis or depiction of events close in time to situations described.

There are four main sections: "Western Europe," "European Union," "Countries of Western Europe," and "Famous People." Of these, "Countries of Western Europe" is the most extensive. It provides, for most states, works grouped under some or all of the following headings: Art, Colonialism, Economics, European Community Relations, Foreign Relations, Georgraphy, History, Immigration, Language, Literature, Music, Politics and Government, and Religion. These subject areas are expanded in the sections titled "Western Europe" and "European Union" to include a broader and more detailed range of topics. Examples are the following: Agriculture, Banks and Banking, Cold War, Environmental Policy, Ethnicity, Human Rights, and Linguistic Minorities. An effort has been made in all sections to list works concerned with two important engines of societal change—multiculturalism and the changing status of women.

Citations were culled through the extensive examination of research collections, journals, bibliographies, publishers lists, and the SCORPIO and MUMS databases of the Library of Congress. For a further examination of individual countries, please consult the relevant volumes in the Scarecrow European Historical Dictionaries series.

I wish to express sincere appreciation to David Kraus, assistant chief, European Division, Library of Congress, and to Jon Woronoff, series editor, for their close readings of this bibliography and their valuable comments and suggestions. All faults of inclusion or omission are, of course, entirely my own. To my mother Florence Salick Higbee go profound thanks for having encouraged, at an early age, a life-long interest in Western Europe.

Europe

Europe—Agriculture

1. Alexandratos, Nikos, ed. *European Agriculture*. London and New York: Published by arrangement with the Food and Agriculture Organization of the United Nations by Belhaven Press, 1990.

2. *The Dynamics of Agrarian Structures in Europe*. Rome: Food and Agriculture Organization of the United Nations, 1988.

3. Hathaway, Dale E. *Agriculture and the GATT: Rewriting the Rules.* Policy Analysis in International Economics, no. 20. Washington, D.C.: Institute for International Economics, 1987.

4. Tracy, Michael. *Government and Agriculture in Western Europe, 1880–1988*. 3d ed. New York: New York University Press, 1989.

5. Young, Michael Denis, ed. *Towards Sustainable Agricultural Development*. London and New York: Belhaven Press, 1991.

Europe—Architecture

6. Amsoneit, Wolfgang. *Contemporary European Architects*. Cologne: Benedikt Taschen, 1991.

7. Baer, Norbert Sebastian, C. Sabbioni, and Andre I. Sors, eds. *Science, Technology, and European Cultural Heritage*. Oxford and Boston: Published for the Commission of the European Community by Butterworth-Heinemann, 1991.

8. Lennard, Suzanne H. Crowhurst, and Henry L. Lennard. *Livable Cities: People and Places: Social and Design Principles for the Future of the City*. Southampton, N.Y.: Gondolier Press, 1987.

9. Sachar, Brian. *An Atlas of European Architecture*. New York: Van Nostrand Reinhold, 1984.

10. Tzonis, Alexander, and Liane Lefaivre. *Architecture in Europe Since 1968: Memory and Invention*. New York: Rizzoli, 1992.

11. Whittick, Arnold. *European Architecture in the Twentieth Century.* New York: Abelard-Schuman, 1974.

Europe—Art

12. Bonito Oliva, Achille. *Europe/America: The Different Avant-Gardes.* Milan: Deco Press, 1976.

13. Castagno, John. *European Artists: Signatures and Monograms, 1800–1990.* Metuchen, N.J.: Scarecrow Press, 1990.

14. Cutul, Ann-Marie. *Twentieth-Century European Painting: A Guide to Information Sources.* Art and Architecture Information Guide Series, no. 9. Detroit: Gale Research Co., 1980.

15. Des Moines Art Center. *Art in Western Europe: The Postwar Years, 1945–1955.* Des Moines: The Center, 1978.

16. *European Painting in the Seventies: New Work by Sixteen Artists.* Los Angeles: Los Angeles County Museum of Art, 1975.

17. Godfrey, Tony. *The New Image: Painting in the 1980s.* 1st Abbeville Press ed. New York: Abbeville Press, 1986.

18. *Grafiek uit Benelux=L'Art graphique en Bénélux.* Delft: Centraal Orgaan voor het Scheppend Ambacht, 1979.

19. McCabe, Cynthia Jaffee. *Artistic Collaboration in the Twentieth Century.* Washington, D.C.: Smithsonian Institution Press, 1984.

20. Nicholas, Lynn H. *The Rape of Europa: The Fate of Europe's Treasures in the Third Reich & the Second World War.* New York: Knopf, 1994.

21. Plant, Sadie. *The Most Radical Gesture: The Situationist International in a Postmodern Age.* London and New York: Routledge, 1992.

22. Solomon R. Guggenheim Museum. *Acquisition Priorities: Aspects of Postwar Painting in Europe.* New York: The Museum, 1983.

23. Wexner Center for the Arts. *Breakthroughs: Avant-Garde Artists in Europe and America, 1950–1990.* New York: Rizzoli, 1991.

Europe—Banks and Banking

24. Arestis, Philip, ed. *Money and Banking Issues for the Twenty-First Century.* New York: St. Martin's Press, 1993.

25. De Cecco, Marcello, and Alberto Giovannini, eds. *A European Central Bank?: Perspectives on Monetary Unification After Ten Years of the EMS.* Cambridge and New York: Cambridge University Press, 1989.

26. European Investment Bank. *European Investment Bank: 25 Years, 1958–1983.* Luxembourg: The Bank, 1983.

27. Frazer, William Johnson. *The Central Banks: The International and European Directions.* Forthcoming.

28. Goodman, John B. *Monetary Sovereignty: The Politics of Central Banking in Western Europe.* Ithaca: Cornell University Press, 1992.

29. Hasse, Rolf, Werner Weidenfeld, and Reinhold Biskup. *The European Central Bank: Perspectives for a Further Development of the European Monetary System.* Strategies and Options for the Future of Europe. Basic Findings; no. 2 Gutersloh: Bertelsmann Foundation, 1990. Originally published as *Europäische Zentralbank.*

30. Spirou, Claire. *La Banque européenne d'investissement: aspects juridiques de ses opérations de financement.* Etudes suisses de droit international, no. 61. Zürich: Schulthess, 1990.

31. Weiserbs, Daniel, ed. *Industrial Investment in Europe: Economic Theory and Measurement.* International Studies in Economics and Econometrics, no. 12. Dordrecht and Boston: M. Nijhoff, 1985.

Europe—Benelux

32. Belgium. Ministry of Foreign Affairs and External Trade. *Some Aspects of the Belgium-Luxembourg Economic Union.* Memo from Belgium, no. 40. Brussels: The Ministry, 1963.

33. Chapel, Yves. *Le régime administratif de l'union économique belgo-luxembourgeoise.* Bruxelles: Institut international des sciences administratives, 1958.

34. Gay, François J. *Le Bénélux.* 4e éd. Paris: Presses Universitaires de France, 1970.

35. Hylkema, Edgar. *Bénélux; le chemin vers l'unité économique.* Paris: A. Pedoné, 1948.

36. Leener, Georges de. *L'Union économique hollando-belgo-luxembourgeoise.* Actualités sociales, nouv. sér., no. 11. Bruxelles: Institut de sociologie Solvay, 1945.

37. Mansfield, Anthony John, P. J. Powrie, and Kenneth Eifion Williams. *France and Benelux.* London: Harrap, 1972.

38. Stein, George. *Benelux Security Cooperation: A New European Defense Community?* Boulder: Westview, 1990.

Europe—Berlin Blockade

39. Collier, Richard. *Bridge Across the Sky: The Berlin Blockade and Airlift, 1948–1949.* New York: McGraw-Hill, 1978.

40. Davison, Walter Phillips. *The Berlin Blockade: A Study in Cold War Politics.* Dissertations on Sociology. New York: Arno Press, 1980.

41. Shlaim, Avi. *The United States and the Berlin Blockade, 1948– 1949: A Study in Crisis Decision-Making.* Berkeley: University of California Press, 1983.

42. Tusa, Ann, and John Tusa. *The Berlin Blockade.* London: Hodder & Stoughton, 1988.

Europe—Cinema

43. Dyer, Richard, and Ginette Vincendeau, eds. *Popular European Cinema.* London and New York: Routledge, 1992.

44. Lev, Peter. *The Euro-American Cinema.* Texas Film Studies Series. Austin: University of Texas Press, 1993.

45. Lovell, Alan, ed. *Art of the Cinema in Ten European Countries.* Education in Europe. Section 4: General, no. 7. Strasbourg: Council of Europe, 1967.

46. Petrie, Duncan, ed. *Screening Europe: Image and Identity in Contemporary European Cinema.* London: BFI Pub., 1992.

47. Segrave, Kerry, and Linda Martin. *The Continental Actress: European Film Stars of the Postwar Era.* Jefferson, N.C.: McFarland, 1990.

Europe—Cold War

48. Allan, Pierre, and Goldmann, Kjell, eds. *The End of the Cold War: Evaluating Theories of International Relations.* Dordrecht and Boston: M. Nijhoff, 1992.

49. Brandon, Henry, ed. *In Search of a New World Order: The Future of U.S.-European Relations.* Washington, D.C.: Brookings Institution, 1992.

50. Deighton, Anne. *The Impossible Peace: Britain, the Division of Germany and the Origins of the Cold War.* Oxford: Clarendon Press; and New York: Oxford University Press, 1990.

51. Dunbabin, John. *International Relations Since 1945.* 2 vols. Forthcoming.

52. Frankel, Benjamin, ed. *The Cold War, 1945–1991.* 3 vols. Detroit: Gale Research, 1992.

53. Freedman, Lawrence, ed. *Europe Transformed: Documents on the End of the Cold War*. New York: St. Martin's Press, 1990.

54. Gordon, Philip H. *A Certain Idea of France: French Security Policy and the Gaullist Legacy*. Princeton Studies in International History and Politics. Princeton: Princeton University Press, 1993.

55. Hewison, Robert. *In Anger: British Culture in the Cold War, 1945–1960*. 1st American ed. New York: Oxford University Press, 1981.

56. Hogan, Michael J., ed. *The End of the Cold War: Its Meaning and Implications*. Cambridge and New York: Cambridge University Press, 1992.

57. Horowitz, David, ed. *Containment and Revolution: Western Policy Towards Social Revolution: 1917 to Vietnam*. Studies in Imperialism and the Cold War, no. 1. London: Blond, 1967.

58. Kent, John. *British Imperial Strategy and the Origins of the Cold War, 1944–49*. Leicester and New York: Leicester University Press, 1993.

59. Kofas, Jon V. *Intervention and Underdevelopment: Greece During the Cold War*. University Park: Pennsylvania State University Press, 1989.

60. Krell, Gert, ed. *Searching for Peace After the Cold War: Conceptual and Practical Problems of a New European Peace Order*. PRIF Reports, no. 19–20. Frankfurt am Main: Peace Research Institute Frankfurt, 1991.

61. Leffler, Melvyn P., and David S. Painter, eds. *Origins of the Cold War: An International History*. London and New York: Routledge, 1994.

62. Qasim Ahmad. *Britain, Franco Spain, and the Cold War, 1945–1950*. Modern European History. London and New York: Garland, 1992.

63. Ryan, Henry Butterfield. *The Vision of Anglo-America: The US-UK Alliance and the Emerging Cold War, 1943–1946*. Cambridge and New York: Cambridge University Press, 1987.

64. Weiler, Peter. *British Labour and the Cold War*. Stanford: Stanford University Press, 1988.

65. Young, John W. *France, the Cold War, and the Western Alliance, 1944–49: French Foreign Policy and Post-War Europe*. New York: St. Martin's Press, 1990.

Europe—Conference on Security and Cooperation in Europe (CSCE)

66. Bloed, Arie, ed. *From Helsinki to Vienna: Basic Documents of the Helsinki Process*. Dordrecht and Boston: M. Nijhoff in co-operation with the Europa Instituut, Utrecht, 1990.

67. Cuthbertson, Ian M., ed. *Redefining the CSCE: Challenges and Opportunities in the New Europe.* Special Report. New York: Institute for East West Studies; and Helsinki: Finnish Institute of International Affairs, 1992.

68. Fry, John. *The Helsinki Process: Negotiating Security and Cooperation in Europe.* Washington, D.C.: National Defense University Press, 1993.

69. Lehne, Stefan. *The Vienna Meeting of the Conference on Security and Cooperation in Europe, 1986–1989: A Turning Point in East-West Relations.* Austrian Institute for International Affairs Series. Boulder: Westview Press, 1991.

70. Lucas, Michael R. *The Conference on Security and Cooperation in Europe and the Post-Cold War Era.* Hamburger Beiträge zur Friedensforschung und Sicherheitspolitik, Heft 48. Hamburg: Institut für Friedensforschung und Sicherheitspolitik, 1990.

71. Mastny, Vojtĕch. *The Helsinki Process and the Reintegration of Europe, 1986–1991: Analysis and Documentation.* New York: New York University Press, 1992.

72. Rotfeld, Adam Daniel, ed. *From Helsinki to Helsinki and Beyond: Analysis and Documents of the Conference on Security and Cooperation in Europe, 1973–93.* Forthcoming.

73. Wells, Samuel F., ed. *The Helsinki Process and the Future of Europe.* Woodrow Wilson Center Special Studies, no. 1. Washington, D.C.: Wilson Center Press, 1990.

Europe—Council of Europe

74. Betten, Lammy. *The Future of European Social Policy.* 2d ed. European Monographs, no. 1. Deventer and Boston: Kluwer Law and Taxation Publishers, 1991.

75. Council of Europe. *The Council of Europe: A Guide.* Strasbourg: Directorate of Press and Information on the Council of Europe, 1986.

76. Council of Europe. *General Agreement on Privileges and Immunities of the Council of Europe of 2nd September 1949, together with the Supplementary Agreement of 18th March 1950, the Protocol to the General Agreement of 6th November 1952, the Second Protocol of 15th December 1956, the Third Protocol of 6th March 1959, and the Fourth Protocol of 16th December 1961.* Strasbourg: The Council, 1971.

77. Council of Europe. Secretariat. *Manual of the Council of Europe: Structure, Functions and Achievements.* London: Stevens; and South Hackensack, N.J.: Rothman, 1970.

78. Harris, David John. *The European Social Charter.* Procedural Aspects of International Law Series, no. 17. Charlottesville: University Press of Virginia, 1984.

79. Medefind, Heinz. *Organisation Europe: The Eighteen and the Nine and Among Them the Germans: The Development, Chances, Limitations of the European Institutions.* Bonn: Europa Union Verlag, 1975. Originally published as: Organisation Europa.

80. Robertson, Arthur Henry. *The Relations Between the Council of Europe and The United Nations.* United Nations Institute for Training and Research. UNITAR Regional Study, no. 1. New York: UNITAR, 1972.

Europe—Cultural Policy

81. Bianchini, Franco, and Michael Parkinson, eds. *Cultural Policy and Urban Regeneration: The West European Experience.* Manchester and New York: Manchester University Press, 1993.

82. Centre for Cultural Research (Bonn). *Handbook of Cultural Affairs in Europe.* Baden-Baden: Nomos Verlagsgesellschaft, 1985.

83. Colloquy on European Law (13th: 1983: Delphoi, Greece). *International Legal Protection of Cultural Property.* Strasbourg: Council of Europe, 1984.

84. Langsted, Jorn, ed. *Strategies: Studies in Modern Cultural Policy.* Aarhus, Denmark: Aarhus University Press, 1990.

85. Shaughnessy, Haydn, and Carmen Fuente Cobo. *The Cultural Obligations of Broadcasting: National and Transnational Legislation Concerning Cultural Duties of Television Broadcasters in Europe.* Media Monograph, no. 12. Manchester: European Institute for the Media, 1990.

Europe—Decolonization

86. Dixon, Chris, and Michael Heffernan, eds. *Colonialism and Development in the Contemporary World.* London and New York: Mansell, 1991.

87. Grimal, Henri. *Decolonization: The British, French, Dutch, and Belgian Empires, 1919–1963.* Translated by Stephan De Vos. London: Routledge & Kegan Paul, 1978.

88. Holland, Robert F. *European Decolonization, 1918–1981: An Introductory Survey.* Themes in Comparative History. Houndsmills, Basingstoke: Macmillan, 1985.

89. Kahler, Miles. *Decolonization in Britain and France: The Domestic Consequences of International Relations.* Princeton: Princeton University Press, 1984.

90. Kent, John. *The Internationalization of Colonialism: Britain, France, and Black Africa, 1939–1956.* Oxford Studies in African Affairs. Oxford: Clarendon Press; and New York: Oxford University Press, 1992.

91. Kiernan, Victor Gordon. *From Conquest to Collapse: European Empires From 1815 to 1960.* 1st American ed. New York: Pantheon Books, 1982.

Europe—Economic Conditions

92. *The Book of European Forecasts.* London: Euromonitor, 1992.

93. Erikson, Robert, and John H. Goldthorpe. *The Constant Flux: A Study of Class Mobility in Industrial Societies.* Oxford: Clarendon Press; and New York: Oxford University Press, 1992.

94. Johnson, Peter, ed. *European Industries: Structure, Conduct, and Performance.* Aldershot, Hampshire, and Brookfield, Vt.: E. Elgar, 1993.

95. Liesner, Thelma. *One Hundred Years of Economic Statistics.* Rev. and expanded to 1987. New York: Facts on File, 1989.

96. Masser, Ian, Ove Sviden, and Michael Wegener. *The Geography of Europe's Futures.* London and New York: Belhaven Press, 1992.

97. Moore, James P. *The World Business Guide to Europe: The Complete Source for U.S. Executives.* New York: World Almanac, 1992.

98. University of Warwick. Business Information Service. *Sources of European Economic and Business Information.* 5th ed. Aldershot, Hampshire, and Brookfield, Vt.: Gower, 1990.

99. Williams, Allan. *The Western European Economy: A Geography of Post-War Development.* Totowa, N.J.: Barnes & Noble, 1987.

Europe—Economic Integration

100. Armand, Louis, and Michel Drancourt. *The European Challenge.* Translated by Patrick Evans. London: Weidenfeld & Nicolson, 1970. Originally published as *Le Pari européen.*

101. Brealey, Mark, and Conor Quigley. *Completing the Internal Market of the European Community.* 2d ed. London and Boston: Graham & Trotman, 1991.

102. Bromberger, Merry, and Serge Bromberger. *Jean Monnet and the United States of Europe.* Translated by Elaïne P. Halperin. New York: Coward-McCann, 1969. Originally published as *Les Coulisses de l'Europe.*

103. Heath, Edward. *Old World, New Horizons: Britain, Europe, and the Atlantic Alliance.* Cambridge: Harvard University Press, 1970.

104. Pollard, Sidney. *European Economic Integration, 1815–1970.* London: Thames and Hudson, 1974.

105. Scitovsky, Tibor. *Economic Theory and Western European Integration.* Stanford Studies in History, Economics, and Political Science, 16. Stanford: Stanford University Press, 1958.

106. Urwin, Derek W. *The Community of Europe: A History of European Integration Since 1945.* 2d ed. The Postwar World. Forthcoming.

Europe—Economic Policy

107. Baldassarri, Mario, and Robert Mundell, eds. *Building the New Europe.* 2 vols. Central Issues in Contemporary Economic Theory and Policy. New York: St. Martin's Press in association with Revista di Politica Economica, SIPI, Rome, 1993.

108. Dyker, David A., ed. *The National Economies of Europe.* London and New York: Longman, 1992.

Europe—Education

109. Aitken, Douglas J. *A New Meaning for Education: Looking at the Europe Region.* Education Studies and Documents, New Ser., no. 58. Paris: Unesco, 1990.

110. Belanger, Paul, Christiana Winter, and Angela Sutton, eds. *Literacy and Basic Education in Europe on the Eve of the 21st Century.* European Meetings on Educational Research, no. 29. Amsterdam and Berwyn, PA: Swets & Zeitlinger, 1992.

111. Council of Europe. Documentation Section. *The Education of Migrant Workers' Children.* Lisse, Netherlands: Swets & Zeitlinger, 1981.

112. Eraut, Michael, ed. *Education and the Information Society: A Challenge for European Policy.* Cassell Council of Europe Series. London: Cassell, 1991.

113. Husen, Torsten, Albert Tuijnman, and W. D. Halls, eds. *Schooling in Modern European Society: A Report of the Academia Europaea.* Oxford and New York: Pergamon, 1992.

114. Jablonska-Skinder, Hanna, Ulrich Teichler, and Matthias Lanzendorfer. *Handbook of Higher Education Diplomas in Europe.* München and New York: K. G. Saur, 1992.

115. Neave, Guy, and Frans A. van Vught, eds. *Prometheus Bound: The Changing Relationship Between Government and Higher Education in Western Europe.* Oxford and New York: Pergamon, 1991.

116. Starkey, Hugh, ed. *Socialisation of School Children and Their Education for Democratic Values and Human Rights.* European Meetings on Educational Research, no. 26. Amsterdam and Berwyn, PA: Swets & Zeitlinger, 1991.

117. Wyatt, John, ed. *Commitment to Higher Education: Seven West European Thinkers on the Essence of the University.* Buckingham and Bristol, PA: Society for Research into Higher Education & Open University Press, 1990.

Europe—The Elderly

118. Clinquet, R. L., and L. vanden Boer, eds. *Economic and Social Implications of Aging in the ECE Region.* Publications of the Netherlands Interdisciplinary Demographic Institute and the Population and Family Study Center, no. 19. The Hague: The Institute; and Brussels: The Center, 1989.

119. Di Gregorio, Silvana, ed. *Social Gerontology: New Directions.* London and New York: Croom Helm, 1987.

120. Jouvenel, Hugues de. *Europe's Aging Population.* Translated by Clare Degenhardt. Guildford: Butterworths, 1989.

121. Regnier, Victor. *Assisted Living Housing for the Elderly: Design Innovations From the United States and Europe.* New York: Van Nostrand Reinhold, 1994.

Europe—Emigration and Immigration

122. Collinson, Sarah. *Europe and International Migration.* London and New York: Pinter Publishers for Royal Institute of International Affairs, 1993.

123. Hollifield, James Frank. *Immigrants, Markets, and States: The Political Economy of Postwar Europe.* Cambridge: Harvard University Press, 1992.

124. Luciani, Giacomo, ed. *Migration Policies in Europe and the United States.* Dordrecht and Boston: Kluwer Academic Publishers, 1993.

125. Power, Jonathan, and Anna Hardman. *Western Europe's Migrant Workers.* 2d rev. ed. Report, no. 28. London: Minority Rights Group, 1984.

126. Rex, John, Daniele Joly, and Czarina Wilpert, eds. *Immigrant Associations in Europe.* Aldershot, Hampshire, and Brookfield, Vt.: Gower, 1987.

127. Wrench, John, and John Solomos, eds. *Racism and Migration in Western Europe.* Oxford; Providence: Berg, 1993.

Europe—Environmental Policy

128. European Conference on Environment and Health (1st: 1989: Frankfurt am Main, Germany). *Environment and Health: The European Charter and Commentary.* Copenhagen: World Health Organization, Regional Office for Europe, 1990.

129. European Trade Union Institute. *Environmental Protection in Europe: Situation and Trade Union Views.* Brussels: G. Kopke, 1992.

130. Haigh, Nigel, and Francis Irwin, eds. *Integrated Pollution Control in Europe and North America.* Washington, D.C.: Conservation Foundation; and Bonn: Institute for European Environmental Policy, 1990.

131. Navrud, Stale, ed. *Pricing the European Environment.* Oslo: Scandinavian University Press; and New York: Oxford University Press, 1992.

132. Pfister, Christian, and Peter Brimblecombe, eds. *The Silent Countdown: Essays in European Environmental History.* Berlin and New York: Springer-Verlag, 1990.

Europe—Ethnicity

133. Amersfoort, Hans van, and Hans Knippenberg, eds. *States and Nations: The Rebirth of the 'Nationalities Question' in Europe.* Nederlandse geografische studies, no. 137. Amsterdam: Koninklijk Nederlandse Aardrijkskundig; Genootschap: Instituut voor Sociale Geografie, Faculteit Ruimtelijke Wetenschapppen, Universiteit van Amsterdam, 1991.

134. Foster, Charles Robert, ed. *Nations without a State: Ethnic Minorities in Western Europe.* New York: Praeger, 1980.

135. Garcia, Soledad, ed. *European Identity and the Search for Legitimacy*. London and New York: Pinter Publishers for the Eleni Nakou Foundation and the Royal Institute of International Affairs, 1993.

136. Howell, David W., Gert von Pistohlkors, and Ellen Wiegandt, eds. *Roots of Rural Ethnic Mobilisation*. Comparative Studies on Governments and Non-Dominant Ethnic Groups in Europe, no. 7. New York: European Science Foundation: New York University Press, 1993.

Europe—European Economic Area (EEA)

137. *Agreement on the European Economic Area*. Luxembourg: Office for Official Publications of the European Communities, 1992.

138. Jacot-Guillarmod, Olivier, ed. *Accord EEE: Commentaires et réflexions=EEA Agreement: Comments and Reflexions*. Collection de droit européen, no. 9. Zürich: Schulthless Polygraphischer; Bern: Stampfli, 1992.

Europe—European Free Trade Association (EFTA)

139. Benoit, Emile. *Europe at Sixes and Sevens: The Common Market, the Free Trade Association, and the United States*. New York: Columbia University Press, 1961.

140. *Convention Establishing the European Free Trade Association: Signed at Stockholm on 4th January 1960, Entered into Force 3rd May 1960*. Geneva: European Free Trade Association, 1963.

141. European Free Trade Association. *The European Free Trade Association*. 3d ed. Geneva: EFTA Secretariat, 1987.

142. Lawisen, Finn, ed. *EFTA and the EC: Implications of 1992*. Professional Papers. Maastricht: European Institute of Public Administration, 1990.

143. Meyer, Frederick Victor. *The European Free-Trade Association*. New York: Praeger, 1960.

144. Penderson, Thomas. *European Union and the EFTA Countries: Enlargement and Integration*. London and New York: Pinter Publishers, 1994.

145. Wahl, Nils. *The Free Trade Agreements Between the EC and EFTA Countries: Their Implementation and Interpretation*. Publications by the Institute for Intellectual Property and Market Law at the Stockholm University; no. 44. Stockholm: Institutet for immaterialratt och marknadsratt vid Stockholms universitet, 1988.

Europe—European Space Agency (ESA)

146. Gibbons, Margaret. *The European Space Agency: Cooperation and Competition in Space.* Genève: Institut universitaire de hautes études internationales, 1986.

147. Longdon, Norman, ed. *The Next Step Forward.* ESA BR, no. 37. Noordwijk, The Netherlands: ESA Publications Div., 1991.

Europe—Federation

148. Beugel, Ernst Hans van der. *From Marshall Aid to Atlantic Partnership.* Amsterdam and New York: Elsevier, 1966.

149. *Europe Unites: The Story of the Campaign for European Unity.* London: Hollis & Carter, 1949.

150. Knorr, Klaus Eugen. *Union of Western Europe, A Third Center of Power?* New Haven: Yale Institute of International Studies, 1948.

151. Lauwerys, Joseph Albert. *The Idea of Europe.* The Lucien Wolf Memorial Lecture, 1950. London: Jewish Historial Society of England, 1951.

152. Robertson, Arthur Henry. *European Institutions: Co-operation, Integration, Unification.* The Library of World Affairs; no. 44. London: Stevens, 1959.

153. Zurcher, Arnold John. *The Struggle to Unite Europe, 1940–1958.* New York: New York University Press, 1958.

Europe—Festivals

154. Boissevain, Jeremy, ed. *Revitalizing European Rituals.* London and New York: Routledge, 1992.

155. Johnson, Margaret M. *Festival Europe: Fairs & Celebrations Throughout Europe.* Memphis: Mustang Pub., 1992.

Europe—Foreign Relations

156. Allen, David, and Alfred Pijpers, eds. *European Foreign Policy-Making and the Arab-Israeli Conflict.* The Hague and Boston: M. Nijhoff, 1984.

157. Bethlen, Steven, and Iván Völgyes, eds. *Europe and the Superpowers: Political, Economic, and Military Policies of the 1980s.* Boulder: Westview Press, 1985.

158. Birrenbach, Kurt. *The Future of the Atlantic Community*. New York: Praeger, 1963. Originally published as *Die Zukunft der atlantischen Gemeinschaft*.

159. Collins, Michael J. *Western European Integration: Implications for U.S. Policy and Strategy*. New York: Praeger, 1992.

160. Crawford, Beverly, and Peter W. Schulze, eds. *The New Europe Asserts Itself: A Changing Role in International Relations*. Research Series, no. 77. Berkeley: Institute of International and Area Studies, University of California at Berkeley, 1990.

161. Dahrendorf, Ralf, and Theodore C. Sorensen, eds. *A Widening Atlantic? Domestic Change & Foreign Policy*. Europe/America, no. 4. New York: New York University Press, 1986.

162. Daniels, Gordon, and Reinhard Drifte, eds. *Europe and Japan: Changing Relationships Since 1945*. Woodchurch, Ashford, and Kent: P. Norbury, 1986.

163. DePorte, Anton. *Europe Between the Superpowers: The Enduring Balance*. 2d ed. New Haven: Yale University Press, 1986.

164. Duignan, Peter, and Gann, Lewis H. *The USA and the New Europe, 1945–1993*. Oxford and Cambridge, Mass.: Blackwell, 1994.

165. Eyal, Jonathan. *Europe and Yugoslavia: Lessons from a Failure*. Whitehall Paper Series. London: Royal United Services Institute for Defence Studies, 1993.

166. Greilsammer, Ilan, and Joseph H. H. Weiler, eds. *Europe and Israel: Troubled Neighbours*. Series C—Political and Social Sciences. Berlin and New York: W. De Gruyter, 1988.

167. Grosser, Alfred. *The Western Alliance: European-American Relations Since 1945*. Translated by Michael Shaw. New York: Vintage, 1982. Originally published as *Les occidentaux*.

168. Holland, Martin. *The European Community and South Africa*. London and New York: Pinter Publishers, 1988.

169. Iivonen, Jyrki, ed. *The Changing Soviet Union in the New Europe*. Studies of Communism in Transition. Aldershot, Hampshire, and Brookfield, Vt.: E. Elgar, 1991.

170. Kapur, Harish. *Distant Neighbours: China and Europe*. Publication of the Graduate Institute of International Studies, Geneva, London, and New York: Pinter Publishers, 1990.

171. Mastny, Vojtech. *The Helsinki Process and the Reintegration of Europe, 1986–1991: Analysis and Documentation*. New York: New York University Press, 1992.

172. Neuhold, Hanspeter, ed. *The European Neutrals in the 1990s.* Austrian Institute for International Affairs Series. Boulder: Westview Press, 1992.

173. Shlaim, Avi. *War and Peace in the Middle East.* New York: Whittle Books in association with Viking, 1994.

174. Sutton, Paul, ed. *Europe and the Caribbean.* Warwick University Caribbean Studies. London: Macmillan Caribbean, 1991.

175. Wessell, Nils H., ed. *The New Europe: Revolution in East-West Relations.* Proceedings of the Academy of Political Science, no. 38. New York: Academy of Political Science, 1991.

176. Zartman, I. William, ed. *Europe and Africa: The New Phase.* SAIS African Studies Library. Boulder: L. Rienner, 1993.

Europe—Freedom of Movement

177. Burrows, F. *Free Movement in European Community Law.* Oxford: Clarendon Press; Oxford and New York: Oxford University Press, 1987.

178. Commission of the European Communities. *Freedom of Movement for Persons in the European Community.* European Documentation. Periodical, 3/1982. Luxembourg: Office for Official Publications of the European Communities, 1982.

179. Commission of the European Communities. *Freedom of Movement for Workers within the Community: Official Texts.* Brussels: Commission of the European Communities, 1977.

180. Haase, H. M. J. M. *The Mobility of Cultural Workers Within the Community: Study Carried out for the Commission of the European Communities.* Cultural Matters Series, no. 1. Brussels: Commission of the European Communities, 1975.

181. Hurwitz, Leon. *The Free Circulation of Physicians Within the European Community.* Aldershot, Hampshire, and Brookfield, Vt. Avebury, 1990.

Europe—General Agreement on Tariffs and Trade (GATT)

182. American Tariff League. *The Story Behind GATT: Facts About the General Agreement on Tariffs and Trade and the Organization for Trade Cooperation.* New York: The League, 1955.

183. General Agreement on Tariffs and Trade (1947). *Text of the General Agreement.* Geneva: GATT, 1986.

184. McGovern, Edmond. *International Trade Regulation: GATT, the United States, and the European Community.* 2d ed. Exeter: Globefield Press, 1986.

185. Wiemann, Jurgen. *The Implications of the Uruguay Round and the Single Market for the European Community's Trade Policy Towards Developing Countries*. Occasional Papers of the German Development Institute, GDI, no. 99. Berlin: German Development Institute, 1990.

Europe—Green Movement

186. Group of Green Economists. *Ecological Economics: A Practical Programme for Global Reform*. Translated by Anna Gyorgy. London and Atlantic Highlands, N.J.: Zed Books, 1992. Originally published as *Grünen im Bundestag*.

187. Kamieniecki, Sheldon, ed. *Environmental Politics in the International Arena: Movements, Parties, Organizations, and Policy*. SUNY Series in Environmental Policy. Albany: State University of New York Press, 1993.

188. Parkin, Sara, ed. *Green Light on Europe*. London: Heretic Books, 1991.

189. Pilat, Joseph F. *Ecological Politics: The Rise of the Green Movement*. Beverly Hills: Sage Publications, 1980.

Europe—History

190. Ambrosius, Gerold, and William H. Hubbard. *A Social and Economic History of Twentieth-Century Europe*. Translated by Keith Tribe and William M. Hubbard. Cambridge: Harvard University Press, 1989. Originally published as Sozial und Wirtschaftsgeschichte Europas im 20. Jahrhundert.

191. Barzini, Luigi. *The Europeans*. New York: Penguin, 1984.

192. Gardner, Lloyd C. *Spheres of Influence: The Great Powers Partition Europe, From Munich to Yalta*. Chicago: I. R. Dee, 1993.

193. Gilbert, Martin. *The Second World War: A Complete History*. 1st American ed. New York: H. Holt, 1989.

194. Hughes, Henry Stuart, and James Wilkinson. *Contemporary Europe*. 7th ed. Englewood Cliffs, N.J.: Prentice Hall, 1991.

195. Kleine-Ahlbrandt, William Laird. *Europe Since 1945: From Conflict to Community*. Minneapolis/St. Paul: West, 1993.

196. Kleine-Ahlbrandt, William Laird. *Twentieth-Century European History*. Minneapolis/St. Paul: West, 1993.

197. Laqueur, Walter. *Europe in Our Time, 1945–1992*. New York: Viking, 1992.

198. Laqueur, Walter. *Europe Since Hitler.* London: Weidenfeld & Nicolson, 1970.

199. Mayne, Richard J. *Postwar, the Dawn of Today's Europe.* 1st American ed. New York: Schocken Books, 1983.

200. Mayne, Richard J. *The Recovery of Europe, 1945–1973.* Garden City, N.Y.: Anchor Press, 1973.

201. Mommsen, Wolfgang J., ed. *The Long Way to Europe: Historical Observations From a Contemporary View.* Chicago: Edition Q, 1994. Originally published as *Langer Weg nach Europa.*

202. Mowat, Robert Case. *Creating the European Community.* New York: Barnes & Noble Books, 1973.

203. Rostow, Walt Whitman. *The Division of Europe After World War II, 1946.* Ideas and Action Series. Austin: University of Texas Press, 1981.

204. Urwin, Derek W. *Western Europe since 1945: A Political History.* 4th ed. London and New York: Longman, 1989.

205. Wegs, J. Robert. *Europe Since 1945: A Concise History.* 3d ed. New York: St. Martin's Press, 1991.

Europe—Human Rights

206. Cassese, Antonio, and Andrew Clapham, eds. *Transfrontier Television in Europe: The Human Rights Dimension.* Baden-Baden: Nomos Verlagsgesellschaft, 1990.

207. Clapham, Andrew. *Human Rights in the Private Sphere.* Oxford Monographs in International Law. Oxford: Clarendon Press and New York: Oxford University Press, 1993.

208. Colloquy on "Human Rights of Aliens in Europe" (1983: Funchal, Madeira). *Human Rights of Aliens in Europe.* Dordrecht and Boston, M. Nijhoff, 1985.

209. Council of Europe. *European Convention on Human Rights: Collected Texts.* Dordrecht and Boston: M. Nijhoff, 1987.

210. Council of Europe. *Universality of Human Rights in a Pluralistic World: Proceedings of the Colloquy Organised by the Council of Europe in Co-operation with the International Institute of Human Rights.* Kehl and Arlington, Va.: N. P. Engel, 1990.

211. Council of Europe. Committee of Ministers. *Collection of Recommendations, Resolutions, and Declarations of the Committee of Ministers Concerning Human Rights, 1949–87.* Strasbourg: The Council, 1989.

212. Council of Europe. Secretariat. *Implementation of the European Convention on Human Rights in Respect of Young Persons and Children Placed in Care or in Institutions Following a Decision of the Administration or Judicial Authorities.* Strasbourg: Council of Europe, 1986.

213. Fabricius, Fritz. *Human Rights and European Politics: The Legal-Political Status of Workers in the European Community.* Oxford and New York: Berg, 1992.

214. Macdonald, Ronald, Franz Matscher, and Herbert Petzold, eds. *The European System for the Protection of Human Rights.* Dordrecht and Boston, M. Nijhoff, 1993.

215. Merrills, J. G. *The Development of International Law by the European Court of Human Rights.* 2d ed. Manchester, UK, and New York: Manchester University Press, 1993.

216. Mower, Alfred Glenn. *Regional Human Rights: A Comparative Study of the West European and Inter-American Systems.* Studies in Human Rights, no. 12. New York: Greenwood Press, 1991.

217. Robertson, Arthur Henry, and J. G. Merrills. *Human Rights in Europe: A Study of the European Convention on Human Rights.* 3d ed. Manchester, UK, and New York: Manchester University Press, 1993.

218. Waaldijk, Kees, and Andrew Clapham, eds. *Homosexuality, a European Community Issue: Essays on Lesbian and Gay Rights in European Law and Policy.* International Studies in Human Rights, no. 26. Dordrecht and Boston: M. Nijhoff, 1993.

Europe—Industry and State

219. Bangemann, Martin. *Meeting the Global Challenge: Establishing a Successful European Industrial Policy.* London: Kogan Page, 1992.

220. Dyson, Kenneth, ed. *Local Authorities and New Technologies: The European Dimension.* Bradford Studies in European Politics. London and New York: Croom Helm, 1988.

221. Hart, Jeffrey A. *Rival Capitalists: International Competitiveness in the United States, Japan, and Western Europe.* Cornell Studies in Political Economy. Ithaca: Cornell University Press, 1992.

222. Montagnon, Peter, ed. *European Competition Policy.* Chatham House Papers. London: Royal Institute of International Affairs and New York: Council on Foreign Relations Press, 1990.

223. Nester, William R. *European Power and the Japanese Challenge*. New York: New York University Press, 1993.

224. Warnecke, Steven Joshua, and Ezra N. Suleiman. *Industrial Policy in Western Europe*. New York: Praeger, 1975.

Europe—Languages

225. Adler, Max K. *Welsh and the Other Dying Languages in Europe: A Sociolinguistic Study*. Hamburg: Buske, 1977.

226. Calvet, Louis Jean. *L'Europe et ses langues*. Paris: Plon, 1993.

227. Krantz, Grover S. *Geographical Development of European Languages*. American University Studies. Series XI. Anthropology and Sociology, no. 26. New York: P. Lang, 1988.

Europe—Linguistic Minorities

228. Allardt, Erik. *Implications of the Ethnic Revival in Modern Industrialized Society: A Comparative Study of the Linguistic Minorities in Western Europe*. Commentationes Scientiarum Socialium, no. 12. Helsinki: Societas Scientiarum Fennica, 1979.

229. Coulmas, Florian, ed. *A Language Policy for the European Community: Prospects and Quandaries*. Contributions to the Sociology of Language; no. 61. Berlin and New York: Mouton de Gruyter, 1991.

230. De Marchi, Bruna, and Anna Maria Boileau, eds. *Boundaries and Minorities in Western Europe*. Milan: Franco Angeli, 1982.

231. Extra, Guus, and Ludo Verhoeven, eds. *Immigrant Languages in Europe*. Philadelphia: Multilingual Matters, 1993.

232. Falch, Jean. *Contribution à l'étude du statut des langues en Europe*. Québec: Presses de l'Université Laval, 1973.

233. Istituto della Enciclopedia Italiana. *Linguistic Minorities in Countries Belonging to the European Community*. Luxembourg: Commission of the European Communities, 1986.

234. Ormeling, Ferdinand Jan. *Minority Toponyms on Maps: The Rendering of Linguistic Minority Toponyms on Topographic Maps of Western Europe*. Translated by G. P. Oxtoby. Utrechtse geografische studies, no. 30. Utrecht: Dept. of Geography, University of Utrecht, 1983.

235. Pogarell, Reiner. *Minority Languages in Europe: A Classified Bibliography*. Berlin and New York: Mouton, 1983.

236. Price, Glanville. *The Present Position of Minority Languages in Western Europe: A Selective Bibliography.* Cardiff: University of Wales, 1969.

Europe—Literature

237. Bede, Jean Albert, and William B. Edgerton, eds. *Columbia Dictionary of Modern European Literature.* 2d ed. New York: Columbia University Press, 1980.

238. Demetz, Peter. *After the Fires: Recent Writing in the Germanies, Austria, and Switzerland.* 1st Harvest/HBJ ed. San Diego: Harcourt Brace Jovanovich, 1992.

239. Harris, Frederick John. *Encounters with Darkness: French and German Writers on World War II.* New York: Oxford University Press, 1983.

240. Hewitt, Nicholas, ed. *The Culture of Reconstruction: European Literature, Thought, and Film, 1945–50.* New York: St. Martin's Press, 1989.

241. Hoyles, John. *The Literary Underground: Writers and the Totalitarian Experience, 1900–1950.* New York: St. Martin's Press, 1991.

242. Jasper, David, and Colin Crowder, eds. *European Literature and Theology in the Twentieth Century.* Studies in Literature and Religion. Houndmills, Basingstoke: Macmillan, 1991.

243. Jordan, Lothar, ed. *Contemporary European Poetry Magazines: A Selected Bibliography.* Münster: Kleinheinrich, 1987. Originally published as *Europäische Poesiezeitschriften der Gegenwart.*

244. Krewson, Margrit Beran. *Contemporary Authors of the German-Speaking Countries of Europe: A Selective Bibliography.* Washington: Library of Congress, 1988.

245. Larsen, Stein Ugelvik, Beatrice Sandberg, and Ronald Speirs, eds. *Fascism and European Literature.* Bern and New York: P. Lang, 1991.

246. Rose, William, and J. Isaacs, eds. *Contemporary Movements in European Literature.* Essay Index Reprint Series. Freeport, N.Y.: Books for Libraries Press, 1968.

247. Suleiman, Susan Rubin. *Subversive Intent: Gender, Politics, and the Avant-Garde.* Cambridge: Harvard University Press, 1990.

248. Timms, Edward, and David Kelley, eds. *Unreal City: Urban Experience in Modern European Literature and Art.* New York: St. Martin's Press, 1985.

Europe—Marshall Plan

249. Carew, Anthony. *Labour Under the Marshall Plan*. Manchester, U.K.: Manchester University Press, 1987.

250. Dulles, Allen Welsh. *The Marshall Plan*. Providence, RI: Berg, 1993.

251. Gimbel, John. *The Origins of the Marshall Plan*. Stanford: Stanford University Press, 1976.

252. Hogan, Michael J. *The Marshall Plan: America, Britain, and the Reconstruction of Western Europe, 1947–1952*. Studies in Economic History and Policy. Cambridge and New York: Cambridge University Press, 1987.

253. Mee, Charles L. *The Marshall Plan: The Launching of the Pax Americana*. New York: Simon and Schuster, 1984.

254. Sanford, William F. *The American Business Community and the European Recovery Program, 1947–1952*. Foreign Economic Policy of the United States. New York: Garland, 1987.

Europe—Monetary Policy

255. Baldassarri, Mario, and Robert Mundell, eds. *Building the New Europe*. 2 vols. Central Issues in Contemporary Economic Theory and Policy. New York: St. Martin's Press in Association with Revista di Politica Economica, 1993.

256. Fair, Donald E., and Christian de Boissieu, eds. *Fiscal Policy, Taxation, and the Financial System in an Increasingly Integrated Europe*. Financial and Monetary Policy Studies, no. 22. Dordrecht and Boston: Kluwer Academic Publishers, 1992.

257. Wihlborg, Clas, Michele Fratianni, and Thomas D. Willett, eds. *Financial Regulation and Monetary Arrangements After 1992*. Contributions to Economic Analysis, no. 204. Amsterdam and New York: North-Holland, 1991.

Europe—Museums

258. Hudson, Kenneth, and Ann Nicholls. *The Cambridge Guide to the Museums of Europe*. Cambridge and New York: Cambridge University Press, 1991.

259. Miles, Roger, and Lauro Zavala, eds. *Towards the Museum of the Future: New European Perspectives*. London and New York: Routledge, 1994.

260. Pearce, Susan, ed. *Museums and Europe 1992*. New Research in Museum Studies, no. 3. London and Atlantic Highlands, NJ: Athlone Press, 1992.

Europe—Music

261. Adelmann, Marianne, ed. *Musical Europe: An Illustrated Guide to Musical Life in 18 European Countries*. New York: Paddington Press, 1974.

262. Hartog, Howard, ed. *European Music in the Twentieth Century*. London: Routledge and Paul, 1957. Reprint. Westport, Conn.: Greenwood Press, 1976.

263. Lang, Paul Henry, and Nathan Broder, eds. *Contemporary Music in Europe: A Comprehensive Survey*. New York: G. Schirmer, 1966.

264. Searle, Humphrey, and Robert Layton. *Britain, Scandinavia and the Netherlands*. Twentieth Century Composers, no. 3. London: Weidenfeld and Nicolson, 1972.

Europe—National Security

265. Abshire, David M., Richard R. Burt, and R. James Woolsey. *The Atlantic Alliance Transformed*. Significant Issues Series; vol. 14, no. 6. Washington, D.C.: Center for Strategic and International Studies, 1992.

266. Aron, Raymond, and Daniel Lerner, eds. *France Defeats the European Defense Community*. New York: Praeger, 1957. Originally published as *La querelle de la CED*.

267. Ausland, John C. *Nordic Security and the Great Powers*. Westview Special Studies in International Security. Boulder: Westview Press, 1986.

268. Crawford, Beverly, ed. *The Future of European Security*. Research Series, no. 84. Berkeley: Center for German and European Studies, University of California at Berkeley, 1992.

269. Fursdon, Edward. *The European Defence Community: A History*. New York: St. Martin's Press, 1980.

270. Gow, James, and James D. D. Smith. *Peace-making, Peace-keeping: European Security and the Yugoslav Wars*. London Defence Studies, no. 11. London: Brassey's for the Center for Defence Studies, 1992.

271. Heller, Francis Howard, and John R. Gillingham, eds. *NATO: The Founding of the Atlantic Alliance and the Integration of Europe.* The Franklin and Eleanor Roosevelt Institute Series on Diplomatic and Economic History, no. 2. New York: St. Martin's Press, 1992.

272. Heuser, Beatrice, and Robert O'Neill, eds. *Securing Peace in Europe, 1945–62.* New York: St. Martin's Press, 1992.

273. Valki, Laszlo, ed. *Changing Threat Perceptions and Military Doctrines.* New York: St. Martin's Press, 1992.

274. Waver, Ole, Barry Buzan, Morten Kelstrup, and Pierre Lemaitre. *Identity, Migration, and the New Security Agenda in Europe.* New York: St. Martin's Press, 1993.

Europe—North Atlantic Treaty Organization (NATO)

275. Acheson, Dean. *Present at the Creation: My Years in the State Department.* London: Hamilton, 1970.

276. Beckett, William Eric. *The North Atlantic Treaty, The Brussels Treaty, and the Charter of the United Nations.* The Library of World Affairs, no. 12. London: Stevens. Published Under the Auspices of the London Institute of World Affairs, 1950.

277. Cahen, Alfred. *The Western European Union and NATO: Building a European Defence Identity Within the Context of Atlantic Solidarity.* Brassey's Atlantic Commentaries, no. 2. London and Washington: Brassey's (UK), 1989.

278. Guertner, Gary L., Robert Haffa, and George Questor. *Conventional Forces and the Future of Deterrence.* Strategic Concepts in National Military Strategy Series. Carlisle Barracks, PA: Strategic Studies Institute, U.S. Army War College, 1992.

279. Klein, Bradley S. *Strategic Studies and World Order.* Cambridge Studies in International Relations, no. 34. Cambridge and New York: Cambridge University Press, 1994.

280. Williams, Phil. *NATO: An Annotated Bibliography.* International Organizations Series, no. 8. New Brunswick, N.J.: Transaction Publishers, c. 1994.

Europe—Nordic Council

281. Nordic Council. *Co-operation Agreements Between the Nordic Countries: A Compilation of Some of the Basic Co-operation Agreements Between Denmark, Finland, Iceland, Norway, and Sweden.* NORD, 1989: 71. Stockholm: Nordic Council, 1989.

282. Nordic Council of Ministers. *Stronger Nordic Countries*. Stockholm: Nordic Council; Kobenhavn: Nordic Council of Ministers, 1989.

283. Nordic Council of Ministers. Secretariat for Nordic Cultural Cooperation. *Nordic Radio and Television Via Satellite: Main Report*. Stockholm: The Secretariat, 1980. Originally published as *Nordisk radio och television via satellit*.

284. Orvik, Nils, ed. *The Scandinavian Allies and the European Community*. European Studies Programme; no. 1/78. Kingston, Ont.: Center for International Relations, Queen's University, 1978.

285. Solem, Erik. *The Nordic Council and Scandinavian Integration*. Praeger Special Studies in International Politics and Government. New York: Praeger, 1977.

286. Turner, Barry, and Gunilla Nordquist. *The Other European Community: Integration and Cooperation in Nordic Europe*. New York: St. Martin's Press, 1982.

287. Wendt, Frantz Wilhelm. *Cooperation in the Nordic Countries: Achievements and Obstacles*. Translated by Geoffrey Dodd. Stockholm: Published for the Nordic Council by Almqvist & Wiksell International, 1981. Originally published as *Nordisk rad 1952–1978*.

Europe—Nordic Issues

288. Allardt, Erik, ed. *Nordic Democracy: Ideas, Issues, and Institutions in Politics, Economy, Education, Social and Cultural Affairs of Denmark, Finland, Iceland, Norway and Sweden*. Copenhagen: Det Danske Selskab, 1981.

289. Almdal, Preben. *Aspects of European Integration: A View of the European Community and the Nordic Countries*. Odense: Odense University Press, 1986.

290. Engellau, Patrik, and Ulf Henning, eds. *Nordic Views and Values*. Stockholm, Sweden: Nordic Council, 1984.

291. *Growth and Integration in a Nordic Perspective*. Helsinki: ETLA; Stockholm: IUI; and Copenhagen: IFF; Bergen: NOI, 1990.

292. Huldt, Bo, and Atis Lejins, eds. *Security in the North: Nordic and Superpower Perceptions*. Conference Papers (The Swedish Institute of International Affairs). Stockholm: The Institute, 1984.

293. Miljan, Toivo. *The Reluctant Europeans: The Attitudes of the Nordic Countries Towards European Integration*. London: C. Hurst, 1977.

294. Orvik, Nils, ed. *The Scandinavian Allies and the European Community*. European Studies Programme, no. 1/78. Kingston, Ont.: Centre for International Relations, Queen's University, 1978.

295. Taylor, William Jesse, and Paul M. Cole, eds. *Nordic Defense: Comparative Decision Making*. Lexington, Mass.: Lexington Books, 1985.

Europe—Political Parties

296. Budge, Ian, and Hans Keman. *Parties and Democracy: Coalition Formation and Government Functioning in Twenty States*. Comparative European Politics. Oxford and New York: Oxford University Press, 1990.

297. Daalder, Hans, ed. *Party Systems in Denmark, Austria, Switzerland, The Netherlands, and Belgium*. New York: St. Martin's Press, 1987.

298. Gunn, Simon. *Revolution of the Right: Europe's New Conservatives*. Transnational Institute Series. London: Pluto Press with the Transnational Institute, 1989.

299. Jacobs, Francis, ed. *Western European Political Parties: A Comprehensive Guide*. Longman International Reference. Harlow, Essex: Longman, 1989.

300. Kirchner, Emil J., ed. *Liberal Parties in Western Europe*. Cambridge and New York: Cambridge University Press, 1988.

301. Laver, Michael, and Norman Schofield. *Multiparty Government: The Politics of Coalition in Europe*. Comparative European Politics. Oxford and New York: Oxford University Press, 1990.

302. McHale, Vincent E., and Sharon Skowronski, eds. *Political Parties of Europe*. The Greenwood Historical Encyclopedia of the World's Political Parties. 2 vols. Westport, Conn.: Greenwood Press, 1983.

303. Mellors, Colin, and Bert Pijnenburg, eds. *Political Parties and Coalitions in European Local Government*. Bradford Studies in European Politics. London and New York: Routledge, 1989.

304. Muller-Rommel, Ferdinand, ed. *New Politics in Western Europe: The Rise and Success of Green Parties and Alternative Lists*. New Directions in Comparative and International Politics. Boulder: Westview Press, 1989.

305. Muller-Rommel, Ferdinand, and Geoffrey Pridham, eds. *Small Parties in Western Europe: Comparative and National Perspectives*. Sage Modern Politics Series, no. 27. London and Newbury Park, Calif.: Sage Publications, 1991.

Europe—Politics and Government

306. Boggs, Carl. *Social Movements and Political Power: Emerging Forms of Radicalism in the West*. Philadelphia: Temple University Press, 1986.

307. Crouch, Colin, and David Marquand, eds. *Towards Greater Europe?: A Continent Without an Iron Curtain*. Oxford and Cambridge, Mass.: Blackwell, 1992.

308. Dalton, Russell J., and Manfred Kuechler, eds. *Challenging the Political Order: New Social and Political Movements in Western Democracies*. Europe and the International Order. New York: Oxford University Press, 1990.

309. Dogan, Mattei, and Richard Rose, eds. *European Politics: A Reader*. Boston: Little, Brown, 1971.

310. Girvin, Brian, ed. *The Transformation of Contemporary Conservatism*. SAGE Modern Politics Series, no. 22. London and Newbury Park, Cal.: SAGE Publications, 1988.

311. Harris, Geoffrey. *The Dark Side of Europe: The Extreme Right Today*. 2d ed. Edinburgh: Edinburgh University Press, 1994.

312. Keohane, Robert Owen, Joseph S. Nye, and Stanley Hoffmann, eds. *After the Cold War: International Institutions and State Strategies in Europe, 1989–1991*. Cambridge: Harvard University Press, 1993.

313. Kitschelt, Herbert. *The Transformation of European Social Democracy*. Cambridge Studies in Comparative Politics. Cambridge and New York: Cambridge University Press, 1994.

314. Kruzel, Joseph, and Michael H. Haltzel, eds. *Between the Blocs: Problems and Prospects for Europe's Neutral and Nonaligned States*. Washington, D.C.: Woodrow Wilson Center Press; and Cambridge: Cambridge University Press, 1989.

315. Lefeber, R., M. Fitzmaurice, and E. W. Vierdag, eds. *The Changing Political Structure of Europe: Aspects of International Law*. Dordrecht and Boston: M. Nijhoff, 1991.

316. Miller, Mark J. *Foreign Workers in Western Europe: An Emerging Political Force*. New York: Praeger, 1981.

317. Ornstein, Norman J., and Perlman, Mark, eds. *Political Power and Social Change: The United States Faces a United Europe*. The AEI Studies, no. 525. Washington, D.C.: AEI Press, 1991.

318. Rees, G. Wyn, ed. *International Politics in Europe: The New Agenda*. London and New York: Routledge, 1993.

319. Rusi, Alpo. *After the Cold War: Europe's New Political Architecture*. New York: St. Martin's Press, 1991.

320. Treverton, Gregory F., ed. *The Shape of the New Europe*. New York: Council on Foreign Relations Press, 1992.

Europe—Potsdam Conference

321. Feis, Herbert. *Between War and Peace: The Potsdam Conference*. Princeton, N.J.: Princeton University Press, 1960.

322. Mee, Charles L. *Meeting at Potsdam*. London: Deutsch, 1975.

Europe—Privacy

323. Council of Europe. Committee of Ministers. *Protection of Personal Data Used for Employment Purposes*. Strasbourg: Council of Europe, 1989.

324. Council of Europe. Directorate of Legal Affairs. *Secrecy and Openness: Individuals, Enterprises, and Public Administrations*. Strasbourg: Council of Europe, 1988.

325. Shoham, Shlomo Gloria, and Francis Rosenstiel, eds. *And He Loved Big Brother: Man, State, and Society in Question*. Houndmills, Basingstoke: Macmillan for Council of Europe, 1985.

Europe—Quality of Work Life

326. Craipeau, Sylvie, and Jean-Claude Marot. *Telework: Impact on Living and Working Conditions*. Dublin: European Foundation for the Improvement of Living and Working Conditions, 1984.

327. European Trade Union Institute. *The Future of Work*. Bruxelles: ETUI, 1990.

328. Fragnière, Gabriel, ed. *The Future of Work: Challenge and Opportunity*. New Patterns in Work and Employment, no. 8. Assen, Netherlands: Published for the European Centre for Work and Society by Van Gorcum, 1984.

329. Hubert, Tony, ed. *Teutons and Travail*. New Patterns in Work and Employment, no. 7. Assen, The Netherlands: Published for the European Centre for Work and Society by Van Gorcum, 1984.

330. Marsden, David, ed. *Pay and Employment in the New Europe*. Aldershot, Hampshire, and Brookfield, Vt.: E. Elgar, 1992.

Europe—Reconstruction

331. Committee of European Economic Cooperation. *Convention for European Economic Co-operation.* Washington, D.C.: Dept. of State, 1948.

332. Diefendorf, Jeffry M., ed. *Rebuilding Europe's Bombed Cities.* New York: St. Martin's Press, 1990.

333. Milward, Alan S. *The Reconstruction of Western Europe, 1945– 51.* Berkeley: University of California Press, 1984.

334. Royal Institute of International Affairs. *Documents on European Recovery and Defence.* London and New York: The Institute, 1949.

Europe—Religion

335. Fitzsimons, Matthew Anthony, ed. *The Catholic Church Today: Western Europe.* International Studies. Notre Dame: University of Notre Dame Press, 1969.

336. Gerholm, Tomas, and Yngve Georg Lithman, eds. *The New Islamic Presence in Western Europe.* London and New York: Mansell, 1988.

337. International Conference—Remembering for the Future (1988: Oxford, England). *Remembering for the Future.* 3 vols. Oxford and New York: Pergamon Press, 1989.

338. Kepel, Gilles. *The Revenge of God: The Resurgence of Islam, Christianity, and Judaism in the Modern World.* Translated by Alan Braley. University Park, Pa.: Pennsylvania State University Press, 1994. Originally published as *La Revanche de Dieu.*

339. Mouriquand, Jacques. *L'Europe des protestants.* Collection "Le Monde in Marche." Paris: J.-C. Lattes, 1993.

340. Shadid, Wasif A., and P. S. van Koningsveld, eds. *The Integration of Islam and Hinduism in Western Europe.* Kampen, the Netherlands: Kok Pharos Pub. House, 1991.

Europe—Research Guides

341. Dillon, Kenneth J. *Scholars' Guide to Washington, D.C. for Central and East European Studies: Albania, Austria, Bulgaria, Czechoslovakia, Germany (FRG & GDR), Greece (Ancient and Modern), Hungary, Poland, Romania, Switzerland, Yugoslavia.* Scholar's Guide to Washington, D.C., no. 5. Washington, D.C.: Smithsonian Institution Press, 1980.

342. Higbee, Joan Florence. *Scholars' Guide to Washington, D.C. for Southwest European Studies: France, Italy (Including Ancient Rome), Malta, Portugal, Spain, the Vatican.* Scholars' Guide to Washington, D.C., no. 13. Washington, D.C.: Wilson Center Press, 1989.

343. Pitschmann, Louis A. *Scholars' Guide to Washington, D.C. for Northwest European Studies: Belgium, Denmark, Finland, Great Britain, Greenland, Iceland, Ireland, Luxembourg, the Netherlands, Norway, Sweden.* Scholars' Guide to Washington, D.C., no. 10. Washington, D.C.: Smithsonian Institution Press, 1984.

Europe—Social Policy

344. Girod, Roger, Patrick de Laubier, and Alan Gladstone, eds. *Social Policy in Western Europe and the USA, 1950–80.* New York: St. Martin's Press, 1985.

345. Greve, Bent, ed. *Social Policy in Europe.* Copenhagen: Danish National Institute of Social Research, 1992.

346. Heidenheimer, Arnold, Hugo Heclo, and Carolyn Teich Adams. *Comparative Public Policy.* 3d ed. New York: St. Martin's Press, 1990.

347. Hurwitz, Leon, ed. *The Harmonization of European Public Policy: Regional Responses to Transnational Challenges.* Contributions in Political Science, no. 98. Westport, Conn.: Greenwood Press, 1983.

348. Jones, Catherine, ed. *New Perspectives on the Welfare State in Europe.* London and New York: Routledge, 1993.

349. Lewis, Jane, ed. *Women and Social Policies in Europe.* Aldershot, Hampshire, and Brookfield, Vt.: E. Elgar, 1993.

350. Mommsen, Wolfgang J., and Wolfgang Mock, eds. *The Emergence of the Welfare State in Britain and Germany: 1850–1950.* London: Croom Helm on behalf of the German Historical Institute, 1981.

351. Peters, Guy B., and Anthony Barker, eds. *Advising West European Governments: Inquiries, Expertise, and Public Policy.* Pittsburgh: University of Pittsburgh Press, 1993.

352. Swaan, Abram de. *In Care of the State.* New York: Oxford University Press, 1988.

353. Wilensky, Harold L., and Lowell Turner. *Democratic Corporatism and Policy Linkages: The Interdependence of Industrial,*

Labor-Market, Incomes, and Social Policies in Eight Countries. Research Series, no. 69. Berkeley: Institute of International Studies, University of California at Berkeley, 1987.

Europe—Sociology

354. Tester, Keith. *The Life and Times of Post Modernity.* London and New York: Routledge, 1993.

355. Tester, Keith. *The Two Sovereigns: Social Contradictions of European Modernity.* London and New York: Routledge, 1992.

356. Turner, Stephen P., and Dirk Kasler, eds. *Sociology Responds to Fascism.* New York: Routledge, 1992.

357. Nedelmann, Birgitta, and Piotr Sztompka, eds. *Sociology in Europe: In Search of Identity.* Berlin and New York: W. De Gruyter, 1993.

Europe—Technological Innovations

358. Cozijnsen, Anton, and Willem Vrakking, eds. *Handbook of Innovation Management.* Oxford and Cambridge, Mass.: Blackwell Business, 1993.

359. Tulder, Rob van, and Gerd Junne. *European Multinationals in Core Technologies.* Wiley/IRM Series on Multinationals. Chichester and New York: Wiley, 1988.

Europe—Telecommunication

360. Muskens, George, and Jacob Gruppelaar, eds. *Global Telecommunication Networks.* Dordrecht and Boston: Kluwer Academic Publishers for the Commission of the European Communities, 1988.

361. Noam, Eli M. *Telecommunications in Europe.* Communication and Society. New York: Oxford University Press, 1992.

362. Sandholtz, Wayne. *High-Tech Europe.* Studies in International Political Economy. Berkeley: University of California Press, 1992.

363. Tydeman, John, and Ellen Jakes Kelm. *New Media in Europe: Satellites, Cable, VCRs and Videotext.* London and New York: McGraw-Hill, 1986.

Europe—Terrorism

364. Alexander, Yonah, and Dennis A. Pluchinsky, eds. *Europe's Red Terrorists: The Fighting Communist Organizations.* London and Portland, Or.: F. Cass, 1992.

365. Gal-Or, Noemi. *International Cooperation to Suppress Terrorism.* New York: St. Martin's Press, 1985.

366. Gal-Or, Noemi, ed. *Tolerating Terrorism in the West: An International Survey.* London and New York: Routledge, 1991.

367. Gutteridge, William, ed. *Contemporary Terrorism.* New York: Facts on File, 1986.

368. Hamon, Alain, and Jean-Charles Marchand. *Action directe: du terrorisme français à l'euroterrorisme. L'Epreuve des faits.* Paris: Seuil, 1986.

369. Hoffman, Bruce. *Right-Wing Terrorism in Europe.* A Rand Note, N-1856-AF. Santa Monica: Rand Corp., 1982.

370. Moxon-Browne, Edward, ed. *European Terrorism.* International Library of Terrorism, no. 3. Forthcoming.

371. Schmid, Alex Peter, and Ronald D. Crelinsten, eds. *Western Responses to Terrorism.* London and Portland, Or.: F. Cass, 1993.

372. Tucker, H. H., ed. *Combating the Terrorists: Democratic Responses to Political Violence.* New York: Facts on File, 1988.

373. Vercher, Antonio. *Terrorism in Europe: An International Comparative Legal Analysis.* Oxford: Clarendon Press; and New York: Oxford University Press, 1992.

Europe—Transportation

374. Degli Abbati, Carlo. *Transport and European Integration.* European Perspectives Series. Brussels: Commission of the European Communities, 1987.

375. Giannopoulos, G., and A. Gillespie, eds. *Transport and Communications Innovation in Europe.* London and New York: Belhaven Press; New York: Co-published in the Americas with Halsted Press, 1993.

376. Holliday, Ian, Gerard Marcou, and Roger Vickerman. *The Channel Tunnel: Public Policy, Regional Development, and European Integration.* London and New York: Belhaven Press, 1991.

377. Salomon, Ilan, Piet Bovy, and Jean-Pierre Orfeuil, eds. *A Billion Trips a Day: Tradition and Transition in European Travel Patterns.* Transportation, Research, Economics, and Policy, no. 1. Dordrecht and Boston: Kluwer Academic Publishers, 1993.

Europe—Unemployment

378. Commission on Employment Issues in Europe. *A Programme for Full Employment in the 1990s: Report of the Kreisky Commission on Employment in Europe.* Oxford and New York: Pergamon Press, 1989.

379. Dreze, Jacques H., and Charles R. Bean, eds. *Europe's Unemployment Problem.* Cambridge: MIT Press, 1990.

380. Holmlund, Bertil, and Karl-Gustaf Lofgren, eds. *Unemployment and Wage Determination in Europe.* Oxford and Cambridge, Mass.: Blackwell, 1990.

Europe—Value Added Tax (VAT)

381. National Economic Development Office. *Value Added Tax.* London: H.M.S.O., 1971.

382. Tait, Alan A. *Value Added Tax.* McGraw-Hill European Series in Management. London and New York: McGraw-Hill, 1972.

Europe—Violence

383. Bjorgo, Tore, and Rob Witte, eds. *Racist Violence in Europe.* New York: St. Martin's Press; and Houndmills, Basingstoke: Macmillan, 1993.

384. Mommsen, Wolfgang J., and Gerhard Hirschfeld, eds. *Social Protest, Violence, and Terror in Nineteenth- and Twentieth-Century Europe.* New York: St. Martin's Press for the German Historical Institute, London, 1982.

Europe—Western European Union (WEU)

385. Cahen, Alfred. *The Western European Union and NATO: Building a European Defence Identity Within the Context of Atlantic Solidarity.* Brassey's Atlantic Commentaries, no. 2. London and Washington: Brassey's (UK), 1989.

386. Tsakaloyannis, Panos, ed. *The Reactivation of the Western European Union: The Effects on the EC and its Institutions.* Working Papers. Maastricht: European Institute of Public Administration, 1985.

387. Western European Union. *Brussels Treaty as Amended by the Protocol Modifying and Completing the Brussels Treaty.* London: Secretariat-General of the Western European Union, 1958.

Europe—Women

388. Bock, Gisela, and Pat Thane, eds. *Maternity and Gender Policies: Women and the Rise of the European Welfare States, 1880–1950s.* London and New York: Routledge, 1991.

389. Bradshaw, Jan, ed. *The Women's Liberation Movement: Europe and North America.* Oxford and New York: Pergamon Press, 1982.

390. Council of Europe. Directorate of Information. *Council of Europe Activities to Further Women's Interests.* Strasbourg: Directorate of Press and Information, Council of Europe, 1975.

391. Ellis, Evelyn. *European Community Sex Equality Law.* Oxford European Community Law Series. Oxford: Clarendon Press; and New York: Oxford University Press, 1991.

392. Githens, Marianne, Pippa Norris, and Joni Lovenduski, eds. *Different Roles, Different Voices: Women and Politics in the United States and Europe.* New York: HarperCollins College, 1994.

393. Kaplan, Gisela. *Contemporary Western European Feminism.* New York: New York University Press, 1992.

394. Katzenstein, Mary Fainsod, and Carol McClurg Mueller, eds. *The Women's Movements of the United States and Western Europe: Consciousness, Political Opportunity, and Public Policy.* Women in the Political Economy. Philadelphia: Temple University Press, 1987.

395. Lovenduski, Joni. *Women and European Politics: Contemporary Feminism and Public Policy.* Brighton, Sussex: Wheatsheaf Books, 1986.

396. Riffault, Helene. *European Women in Paid Employment: Their Perception of Discrimination at Work.* Brussels: Commission of the European Community, 1980.

397. Snyder, Paula. *The European Women's Almanac.* New York: Columbia University Press, 1992.

398. Vallance, Elizabeth, and Elizabeth Davies. *Women of Europe: Women MEPs and Equality Policy.* Cambridge and New York: Cambridge University Press, 1986.

European Union

European Union—Agriculture

399. Duchène, François, Edward Szczepanik, and Wilfrid Legg. *New Limits on European Agriculture: Politics and the Common Agricultural Policy*. An Atlantic Institute for International Affairs Research Volume. Totowa, N.J.: Rowman & Allanheld, 1985.

400. Fennell, Rosemary. *The Common Agricultural Policy of the European Community: Its Institutional and Administrative Organisation*. 2d ed. Oxford and Boston: BSP Professional Books, 1987.

401. Hill, Brian E. *The Common Agricultural Policy: Past, Present, and Future*. The Methuen EEC Series. London and New York: Methuen, 1984.

402. Neville-Rolfe, Edmund. *The Politics of Agriculture in the European Community*. London: European Centre for Policy Studies, 1984.

European Union—Banks and Banking

403. Arestis, Philip, ed. *Money and Banking: Issues for the Twenty-First Century*. New York: St. Martin's Press, 1993.

404. Cranston, Ross, ed. *The Single Market and the Law of Banking*. London and New York: Lloyd's of London Press, 1991.

405. De Cecco, Marcello, and Alberto Giovannini, eds. *A European Central Bank? Perspectives on Monetary Unification After Ten Years of the EMS*. Cambridge and New York: Cambridge University Press, 1989.

European Union—Bibliography

406. Commission of the European Communities. General Archives. *Inventory of the Historical Archives*. Luxembourg: Office for Official Publications of the European Communities, 1985.

407. Neilson, June. *Reports of the European Communities, 1952–1977: An Index to Authors and Chairmen*. London: Mansell, 1981.

408. Paxton, John. *European Communities*. International Organizations Series, no. 1. New Brunswick, N.J.: Transaction Publishers, 1992.

409. Thomson, Ian. *The Documentation of the European Communities: A Guide*. London and New York: Mansell, 1989.

European Union—Budget

410. Strasser, Daniel. *The Finances of Europe: The Budgetary and Financial Law of the European Communities*. 7th ed. European Perspectives. Luxembourg: Office for Official Publications of the European Communities, 1992.

411. Wildavsky, Aaron, and Eduardo Zapico-Goni, eds. *National Budgeting for Economic and Monetary Union*. Dordrecht and Boston: M. Nijhoff, 1993.

European Union—Council of the European Communities

412. Council of the European Communities. Information Service. *The Council of the European Community: An Introduction to its Structures and Activities*. Luxembourg: Office for Official Publications of the European Communities, 1990.

413. De Bassompierre, Guy. *Changing the Guard in Brussels: An Insider's View of the EC Presidency*. The Washington Papers, no. 135. New York: Praeger, 1988.

414. Kirchner, Emil Joseph. *Decision-Making in the European Community: The Council Presidency and European Integration*. Manchester, U.K., and New York: Manchester University Press, 1992.

415. O'Nuallain, Colm, and Jean-Marc Hoscheit, eds. *The Presidency of the European Council of Ministers: Impacts and Implications for National Governments*. London and Dover, N.H.: Croom Helm, 1985.

European Union—Court of Justice of the European Communities

416. Bengoetxea, Joxerramon. *The Legal Reasoning of the European Court of Justice: Towards a European Jurisprudence*. Oxford: Clarendon Press; and New York: Oxford University Press, 1993.

417. Brown, Lionel Neville, and Francis G. Jacobs. *The Court of Justice of the European Communities*. 3d ed. Modern Legal Studies. London: Sweet & Maxwell, 1989.

418. Scheingold, Stuart A. *The Rule of Law in European Integration: The Path of the Schuman Plan*. Westport, Conn.: Greenwood Press, 1976.

European Union—Directories and Dictionaries

419. Cox, Andrew W., and Paul Furlong. *A Modern Companion to the European Community: A Guide to Key Facts, Institutions, and Terms.* Aldershot, Hampshire: E. Elgar, 1992.

420. Dinan, Desmond. *Historical Dictionary of the European Community.* International Organization Series, no. 1. Metuchen, N.J.: Scarecrow Press, 1993.

421. Morris, Brian, and Klaus Boehm. *The European Community: A Practical Directory and Guide for Business, Industry, and Trade.* 2d ed. Detroit: Gale Research Co., 1986.

422. Paxton, John. *A Dictionary of the European Communities.* 2d ed. New York: St. Martin's Press, 1982.

423. Ramsay, Anne. *Eurojargon: A Dictionary of EEC Acronyns, Abbreviations, and Sobriquets.* 2d ed. Stamford: Capital Planning Information, 1989.

424. Urwin, Derek W. *Historical Dictionary of European Organizations.* International Organizations, no. 4. Metuchen, N.J.: Scarecrow Press, 1944.

European Union—Drugs

425. Flood, Susan, ed. *Illicit Drugs and Organized Crime: Issues for a Unified Europe.* Chicago: Office of International Criminal Justice, The University of Illinois at Chicago, 1991.

European Union—Economic Policy

426. Coffey, Peter, ed. *Main Economic Policy Areas of the ECC. Towards 1992: The Challenge to the Community's Economic Policies When the "Real" Common Market is Created by the End of 1992.* 3d rev. ed. International Studies in Economics and Econometrics, no. 20. Dordrecht and Boston: Kluwer Academic, 1990.

427. Swann, Dennis, ed. *The Single European Market and Beyond: A Study of the Wider Implications of the Single European Act.* London and New York: Routledge, 1992.

European Union—Environmental Policy

428. Bennett, Graham, ed. *Air Pollution Control in the European Community: Implementation of the EC Directives in the Twelve Member States.* International Environmental Law and Policy Series. London and Boston: Graham & Trotman, 1991.

429. Conrad, Jobst. *Options and Restrictions of Environmental Policy on Agriculture.* Nomos Universitätsschriften. Politik, Bd 18. Baden-Baden: Nomos, 1991.

430. Johnson, Stanley P., and Guy Corcelle. *The Environmental Policy of the European Communities.* Brookfield, Vt.: E. Elgar, 1992.

431. Joyce, Frank E., and Gunter Schneider, eds. *Environment and Economic Development in the Regions of the European Community.* Brookfield, Vt.: Avebury, 1989.

432. Press, Alison, and Catherine Taylor. *Europe and the Environment: The European Community and Environmental Policy.* London: Industrial Society, 1990.

433. Weale, Albert. *The New Politics of Pollution.* Issues in Environmental Politics. Manchester, U.K., and New York: Manchester University Press, 1992.

European Union — European Atomic Energy Community (EURATOM)

434. Howlett, Darryl A. *EURATOM and Nuclear Safeguards.* New York: St. Martin's Press, 1990.

435. Pirotte, Olivier. *Trente ans d'expérience Euratom: la naissance d'une Europe nucléaire.* Organisation internationale et relations internationales, no. 17. Bruxelles: E. Bruylant, 1988.

436. *Treaty Establishing the European Atomic Energy Community (Euratom): Rome, 25th March, 1957.* London: H.M.S.O., 1962.

European Union — Europe 1992

437. *Growth and Integration in a Nordic Perspective.* Helsinki: ETLA; Stockholm: IUI; and Copenhagen: IFF; Bergen: NOI, 1990.

438. Ishikawa, Kenjiro. *Japan and the Challenge of Europe 1992.* London and New York: Pinter Publishers for the Royal Institute of International Affairs, 1990.

439. Mayes, David G. *Public Interest and Market Pressures: Problems Posed by Europe 1992.* Basingstoke: Macmillan; and New York: St. Martin's Press, 1993.

440. Obasanjo, Olusegun, and Hans d'Orville, eds. *The Impact of Europe 1992 on West Africa.* New York: C. Russak, 1990.

441. Portes, Richard. *The EC and Eastern Europe After 1992.* London: Centre for European Policy Research, 1990.

442. Springer, Beverly. *The Social Dimension of 1992: Europe Faces a New EC*. New York: Praeger, 1992.

443. Wallace, Cynthia Day, and John M. Kline. *EC 92 and Changing Global Investment Patterns: Implications for the U.S.-EC Relationship*. Significant Issues Series, vol. 14, no. 10. Washington, D.C.: Center for Strategic and International Studies, 1992.

444. Yannopoulos, George N., ed. *Europe and America, 1992: US-EC Economic Relations and the Single European Market*. Fulbright Papers, no. 10. Manchester, UK, and New York: Manchester University Press in Association with the Fulbright Commission, 1991.

European Union—European Coal and Steel Community (ECSC)

445. Acheson, Dean. *Present at the Creation: My Years in the State Department*. London: Hamilton, 1970.

446. Deutsche Gesellschaft für Auswärtige Politik. Forschungsinstitut. *Bibliographie zum Schumanplan, 1950–1952*. Frankfurt am Main: Deutsche Gesellschaft, 1953.

447. Diebold, William. *The Schuman Plan: A Study in Economic Cooperation, 1950–1959*. New York: Published for the Council on Foreign Relations by Praeger, 1959.

448. Gillingham, John. *Coal, Steel, and the Rebirth of Europe, 1945–1955: The Germans and French from Ruhr Conflict to Economic Community*. Cambridge and New York: Cambridge University Press, 1991.

449. Lavergne, Bernard. *Le plan Schuman: Exposé et critique de sa portée économique et politique*. 2 ed. Paris: L'Année politique et économique, 1952.

European Union—European Council

450. Bulmer, Simon, and Wolfgang Wessels. *The European Council: Decision-Making in European Politics*. London: Macmillan, 1987.

451. Hoscheit, Jean-Marc, and Wolfgang Wessels, eds. *The European Council 1974–1986: Evolution and Prospects*. Professional Paper. Maastricht: European Institute of Public Administration, 1988.

452. Werts, Jan. *The European Council*. Amsterdam and New York: North-Holland, 1992.

European Union—European Defense Community (EDC)

453. Fursdon, Edward. *The European Defense Community: A History.* New York: St. Martin's Press, 1980.

454. McGeehan, Robert. *The German Rearmament Question: American Diplomacy and European Defense After World War II.* Urbana: University of Illinois Press, 1971.

European Union—European Political Cooperation (EPC)

455. Guide to the Archives of the Ministries of Foreign Affairs of the Member States of the European Communities and the European Political Cooperation. Luxembourg: Office for Official Publications of the European Communities, 1989.

456. Hephaistos, Panagiotes. *European Political Cooperation: Towards a Framework of Supranational Diplomacy?* Aldershot, Hampshire, and Brookfield, Vt.: Avebury, 1987.

457. Holland, Martin, ed. *The Future of European Political Cooperation: Essays on Theory and Practice.* New York: St. Martin's Press, 1991.

458. Nuttall, Simon J. *European Political Co-operation.* Oxford: Clarendon Press; and New York: Oxford University Press, 1992.

459. Pijpers, Alfred, Elfriede Regelsberger, and Wolfgang Wessels, eds. *European Political Cooperation in the 1980s: A Common Foreign Policy for Western Europe?* Dordrecht and Boston: published in cooperation with the Trans-European Policy Studies Association by M. Nijhoff, 1988.

European Union—European Strategic Programme of Research and Development in Information Technology (ESPRIT)

460. Hirsch, Bernd, and M. Actis-Dato, eds. *ESPRIT CIM: Design, Engineering, Management, and Control of Production Systems.* Amsterdam and New York: North-Holland, 1987.

461. Steels, Luc, and Brice Lepape, eds. *Enhancing the Knowledge Engineering Process: Contributions From ESPRIT.* Amsterdam and New York: North-Holland, 1992.

European Union—Fiscal Policy

462. Baldassarri, Mario, and Paolo Roberti, eds. *Fiscal Problems in the Single-Market Europe.* Central Issues in Contemporary Economic Theory and Policy. New York: St. Martin's Press, 1994.

463. Canzoneri, Matthew B., Vittorio Grilli, and Paul R. Masson, eds. *Establishing a Central Bank: Issues in Europe and Lessons from the U.S.* Cambridge and New York: Cambridge University Press, 1992.

464. Hockley, Graham C. *Fiscal Policy: An Introduction.* London and New York: Routledge, 1992.

465. Kopits, George, ed. *Tax Harmonization in the European Community: Policy Issues and Analysis.* Occasional Paper; no. 94. Washington, D.C.: International Monetary Fund, 1992.

European Union—Foreign Relations

466. Camps, Miriam. *The European Common Market and American Policy.* Princeton: Center of International Studies, Princeton University, 1956.

467. Clesse, Armand, and Raymond Vernon, eds. *The European Community After 1992: A New Role in World Politics?* Baden-Baden: Nomos, 1991.

468. Coffee, Peter. *The External Relations of the EEC.* London: Macmillan, 1976.

469. Commission of the European Communities. *Guide to the Archives of the Ministries of Foreign Affairs of the Member States of the European Communities and the European Political Cooperation.* Luxembourg: Office for Official Publications of the European Communities, 1989.

470. Cosgrove, Carol Ann, and Kenneth J. Twitchett. *The New International Actors: The United Nations and the European Economic Community.* London: Macmillan, 1970.

471. Edwards, Geoffrey, and Elfriede Regelsberger, eds. *Europe's Global Links: The European Community and Inter-Regional Cooperation.* New York: St. Martin's Press, 1990.

472. Eyal, Jonathan. *Europe and Yugoslavia: Lessons From a Failure.* Whitehall Paper Series, 1993. London: Royal United Services Institute for Defence Studies, 1993.

473. Federal Trust Study Group. *The EC and the Developing Countries: A Policy for the Future.* London: The Trust, 1988.

474. Gautier, Xavier. *L'Europe à l'epreuve des Balkans.* Paris: J. Bertoin, 1992.

475. Gianaris, Nicholas V. *The European Community and the United States: Economic Relations.* New York: Praeger, 1991.

476. Lister, Marjorie. *The European Community and the Developing World: The Role of the Lomé Convention*. Aldershot, Hampshire, and Brookfield, Vt.: Avebury, 1988.

477. Portes, Richard. *The EC and Eastern Europe After 1992*. London: Center for European Policy Research, 1990.

478. Schwok, René. *U.S.-EC Relations in the Post-Cold War Era: Conflict or Partnership?* Boulder: Westview Press, 1991.

479. Shlaim, Avi, and G. Yannopoulos, eds. *The EEC and the Mediterranean Countries*. Cambridge and New York: Cambridge University Press, 1976.

480. Tovias, Alfred. *The European Communities' Single Market: The Challenge of 1992 for Sub-Saharan Africa*. World Bank Discussion Papers, no. 100. Washington, D.C.: The World Bank, 1990.

European Union—Foreign Trade

481. Eeckhout, Piet. *The European Internal Market and International Trade: A Legal Analysis*. Oxford European Community Law Series. Forthcoming.

482. Lasok, Dominik. *The Customs Law of the European Economic Community*. 2d ed. Deventer and Boston: Kluwer Law and Taxation Publishers, 1990.

483. Papaconstantinou, Helen. *Free Trade and Competition in the EEC: Law, Policy, and Practice*. London and New York: Routledge, 1988.

484. Van Bael, Ivo, and Jean-François Bellis. *Anti-Dumping and Other Trade Protection Laws of the EEC*. 2d ed. Bicester, Oxfordshire: CCH Editions, 1990.

485. Williams, Robert, Mark Teagan, and Jose Beneyto. *The World's Largest Market: A Business Guide to Europe, 1992*. New York: American Management Association, 1990.

European Union—General Agreement on Tariffs and Trade (GATT)

486. Hilf, Meinhard, Francis Geoffrey Jacobs, and Ernst-Ulrich Petersmann, eds. *The European Community and GATT*. Studies in Transnational Economic Law, no. 4. Deventer, The Netherlands and Boston: Kluwer, 1986.

487. McGovern, Edmond. *International Trade Regulation: GATT, the United States, and the European Community*. 2d ed. Exeter: Globefield Press, 1986.

European Union — Government and Politics

488. Hay, Richard. *The European Commission and the Administration of the Community.* European Documentation: Periodical 3/1989. Luxembourg: Office for Official Publications of the European Communities, 1989.

489. Hurwitz, Leon. *The European Community and the Management of International Cooperation.* Contributions in Political Science, no. 181. New York: Greenwood Press, 1987.

490. Keohane, Robert Owen, and Stanley Hoffmann, eds. *The New European Community: Decisionmaking and Institutional Change.* Boulder: Westview Press, 1991.

491. Nugent, Neill. *The Government and Politics of the European Union.* Durham: Duke University Press, 1994.

492. Sbragia, Alberta M., ed. *Euro-Politics: Institutions and Policy-making in the New European Community.* Washington, D.C.: Brookings Institution, 1991.

493. Siedentopf, Heinrich, and Jacques Ziller, eds. *Making European Policies Work: The Implementation of Community Legislation in the Member States.* 2 vols. London and Newbury Park, CA: SAGE Publications, 1988.

European Union — History

494. Bliss, Christopher, and Jorge Braga de Macedo, eds. *Unity With Diversity in the European Economy: The Community's Southern Frontier.* Cambridge and New York: Cambridge University Press, 1990.

495. Collins, Doreen. *The European Communities: The Social Policy of the First Phase.* 2 vols. London: M. Robertson, 1975.

496. European Communities. *Opening of the Historical Archives of the European Communities to the Public.* Luxembourg: Office for Official Publications of the European Communities, 1983.

497. Fontaine, Pascal. *Europe, A Fresh Start: The Schuman Declaration, 1950–90.* European Documentation, periodical 3/1990. Luxembourg: Office for Official Publications of the European Communities, 1990.

498. Gorman, Lyn, and Marja-Liisa Kiljunen, eds. *The Enlargement of the European Community: Case-Studies of Greece, Portugal, and Spain.* Studies in the Integration of Western Europe. London: Macmillan, 1983.

499. Henderson, William Otto. *The Genesis of the Common Market.* Chicago: Quadrangle Books, 1962.

500. Laurent, Pierre-Henri, ed. *The European Community After Twenty Years.* The Annals of the American Academy of Political and Social Science, no. 440. Philadelphia: The Academy, 1978.

501. Lipgens, Walter. *History of European Integration.* 2 vols. London: Oxford University Press, 1986.

502. Ludlow, Peter. *Beyond 1992: Europe and its World Partners.* Brussels: Center for European Policy Studies, 1989.

503. Mommsen, Wolfgang J., ed. *The Long Way to Europe: Historical Observations From a Contemporary View.* Chicago: Edition Q, 1994. Originally published as *Langer Weg nach Europa.*

504. Morgan, Roger. *West European Politics Since 1945: The Shaping of the European Community.* London: Batsford, 1972.

505. Nicholson, Frances, and Roger East. *From the Six to the Twelve: The Enlargement of the European Communities.* Keesing's International Studies. Harlow, U.K.: Longman, 1987.

506. Schmitt, Hans A. *The Path to European Union: From the Marshall Plan to the Common Market.* Baton Rouge: Louisiana State University Press, 1962.

507. Tsoukalis, Loukas, ed. *The European Community: Past, Present & Future.* Oxford: Blackwell, 1983.

508. Urwin, Derek W. *The Community of Europe: A History of European Integration Since 1945.* 2d ed. The Postwar World. London and New York: Longman, 1995.

509. Von der Groeben, Hans. *The European Community: The Formative Years: The Struggle to Establish the Common Market and the Political Union (1958–1966).* European Perspective Series. Luxembourg: Office for Official Publications of the European Communities, 1987.

510. Weigall, David, and Peter Stirk, eds. *The Origins and Development of the European Community.* Leicester: Leicester University Press, 1992.

European Union—Law

511. Ellis, Evelyn. *European Community Sex Equality Law.* Oxford European Community Law Series. Oxford: Clarendon Press; and New York: Oxford University Press, 1991.

512. Folsom, Ralph H. *European Community Law*. St. Paul, MN: West, 1991.

513. Green, Nicholas, Trevor Hartley, and John Usher. *The Legal Foundations of the Single European Market*. Oxford: Oxford University Press, 1991.

514. Hopt, Klaus J.; and Eddy Wymeersch, eds. *European Company and Financial Law*. 2d ed. Berlin and New York: Walter de Gruyter, 1994.

515. Lasok, Dominik, and John William Bridge. *Law and Institutions of the European Communities*. London and Austin: Butterworths, 1991.

516. Lasok, Dominik, and Peter A. Stone. *Conflict of Laws in the European Community*. Abingdon: Professional Books, 1987.

517. Maresceau, Marc, ed. *The European Community's Commercial Policy After 1992: The Legal Dimension*. Dordrecht and Boston: M. Nijhoff, 1993.

518. Schwarze, Jurgen, ed. *Legislation for Europe, 1992*. Baden-Baden: Nomos Verlagsgesellschaft, 1989.

European Union—Monetary Policy

519. Baldassarri, Mario, and Robert Mundell, eds. *The Single Market and Monetary Unification*. Building the New Europe, no. 1. New York: St. Martin's Press in association with Rivista de Politica Economica, SIPI, Rome, 1993.

520. Emerson, Michael. *One Market, One Money: An Evaluation of the Potential Benefits and Costs of Forming an Economic and Monetary Union*. Oxford and New York: Oxford University Press, 1992.

521. Grauwe, Paul de. *The Economics of Monetary Integration*. Oxford and New York: Oxford University Press, 1992.

522. Johnson, Christopher, ed. *ECU: The Currency of Europe*. London: Euromoney Books, 1991.

523. Masson, Paul R., and Mark P. Taylor. *Policy Issues in the Operation of Currency Unions*. Cambridge and New York: Cambridge University Press, 1993.

524. Welfens, Paul J. J., ed. *European Monetary Integration: EMS Developments and International Post-Maastricht Perspectives*. 2d ed. Berlin and New York: Springer-Verlag, 1994.

European Union—Political Parties

525. Henig, Stanley, ed. *Political Parties in the European Community.* London: Allen & Unwin, 1979.

526. Oudenhove, Guy van. *The Political Parties in the European Parliament.* Leiden: A. W. Sijthoff, 1965.

European Union—Public Opinion

527. Bocker, Martin. *The Social Psychological Analysis of Attitudes Towards the European Community.* European University Studies. Series VI. Psychology, no. 367. Frankfurt am Main and New York: P. Lang, 1992.

528. Rabier, Jacques-René, Hélène Riffault, and Ronald Inglehart. *Gender Roles in the European Community: April 1983.* 2d ICPSR ed. Euro-barometer, no. 19. Ann Arbor: Inter-University Consortium for Political and Social Research, 1984.

529. Reif, Karlheinz, and Anna Melich. *Immigrants and Out Groups in Western Europe: October-November 1988.* 1st ICPSR ed. Euro-barometer, no. 30. Ann Arbor: Inter-University Consortium for Political and Social Research, 1991.

530. Reif, Karlheinz, and Ronald Inglehart, eds. *Eurobarometer: The Dynamics of European Public Opinion.* New York: St. Martin's Press, 1991.

European Union—Regional Planning

531. *An Empirical Assessment of Factors Shaping Regional Competitiveness in Problem Regions.* 5 vols. Luxembourg: Commission of the European Communities, 1990.

532. Commission of the European Communities. Directorate-General for Regional Policy. *The Regions in the 1990s.* Brussels: Office for Official Publications of the European Communities, 1991.

533. Sweeney, Gerald Patrick. *Innovation, Entrepreneurs, and Regional Development.* New York: St. Martin's Press, 1987.

534. Tykkylainen, Markku. *Development Issues and Strategies in the New Europe: Local, Regional, and Interregional Perspectives.* Aldershot, Hampshire, and Brookfield, Vt.: Avebury, 1992.

European Union—Single European Act (1986) (SEA)

535. Barav, Ami, ed. *Commentary on the EC Treaty and the Single European Act.* Oxford: Clarendon Press, 1993.

536. Carswell, Lucie. *Law & Business in the European Single Market.* International Law, Corporate Law Series. New York: Law Journal Seminars—Press, 1993.

537. Council of the European Communities. *Single European Act and Final Act.* Brussels: The Council, 1986.

European Union—Structure and Institutions

538. *European Communities: 1. European Economic Community (EEC). 2. European Atomic Energy Community (EURATOM). 3. European Coal and Steel Community (ECSC).* Dublin: Stationery Office, 1967.

539. Nicoll, William, and Trevor C. Salmon. *Understanding the New European Community.* New York: Harvester Wheatsheaf, 1994.

540. Noël, Emile. *Working Together: The Institutions of the European Community.* Luxembourg: Office for Official Publications of the European Communities, 1994.

541. Sbragia, Alberta M., ed. *Euro-Politics: Institutions and Policy-making in the "New" European Community.* Washington, D.C.: Brookings Institution, 1991.

542. Tonnerre, Loic. *Les Communautés européennes.* 2 vols. Paris: Eyrolles, 1991.

543. Wilke, Marc, and Helen Wallace. *Subsidiarity: Approaches to Power-Sharing in the EC.* London: RIIA, 1990.

European Union—Treaties

544. *European Communites, Treaties and Related Instruments.* 10 vols. London: H.M.S.O., 1972.

545. Minet, Paul. *Full Text of the Rome Treaty and an ABC of the Common Market.* London: C. Johnson, 1961.

546. *Treaties Establishing the European Communities: Treaties Amending These Treaties: Single European Act: Resolutions, Declarations.* 2 vols. Luxembourg: Office for Official Publications of the European Communities, 1987.

European Union—Treaty on European Union (1992)

547. *The New Treaty on European Union.* 2 vols. Brussels: Belmont European Policy Centre, 1991–1992.

548. Steinberg, James. *"An Ever Closer Union": European Integration and Its Implications for the Future of U.S.-European Relations.* Santa Monica: Rand, 1993.

549. *L'Union européene; Les traités de Rome et de Maastricht: Textes comparés.* Paris: Documentation française, 1992.

Countries of Western Europe

ANDORRA

Andorra—Economics

550. Lluelles Larrosa, Maria Jesus. *La transformacio economica d'Andorra*. Colleccio Clio, no. 11. Barcelona: L'Avenc, 1991.

Andorra—Geography

551. Adellach Baro, Bonaventura, and Ramon Ganyet Sole. *Geografia i diccionari geografic de les Valls d'Andorra*. Andorra la Vella: Conseil Général de les Valls, 1977.

552. Panareda i Clopes, Josep Maria, and Joseph Nuet i Badia. *Atles de Catalunya i d'Andorra*. Barcelona: Editorial Cruilla, 1986.

Andorra—History

553. Armengol, Lidia, Monica Batlle, and Ramon Gual. *Materials per una bibliografia d'Andorra*. Perpignan, France: Institut d'Estudis Andorrans, Centre de Perpinya, 1978.

554. Carrick, Noel. *Andorra*. New York: Chelsea House Publishers, 1988.

555. Palau Marti, Montserrat. *Andorra: Historia, institutions, costums*. Lleida: Virgili & Pages, 1987.

556. Palau Marti, Montserrat. *Andorra, le pays et les hommes*. Paris: G.-P. Maisonneuve et Larose, 1978.

557. Vanderbeke, Clara. *In the Valleys of Andorra*. Translated by Kenneth C. Scoble. Andorra: Casal i Vall, 1964. Originally published as *Au pays des vallées d'Andorre*.

558. *The World and Its Peoples: Spain, Portugal, Andorra, Gibraltar*. New York: Greystone Press, 1969.

Andorra—Politics and Government

559. Institut d'Estudis Andorrans. Centre de Perpinya. Grup Historia. *Institucions Andorranes.* Dossier, no. 2. Perpignan, France: Institut d'Estudis Andorrans, Centre de Perpinya, 1981.

560. Paris Torres, Enric. *Estudi sobre les institucions andorranes: Organitzacio politico-administrativa, organitzacio judicial.* Andorra la Vella: Conseil Général de les Valls, 1980.

AUSTRIA

Austria—Architecture

561. Zukowsky, John, and Ian Wardropper. *Austrian Architecture and Design: Beyond Tradition in the 1990s.* Chicago: Art Institute of Chicago; Berlin: Ernst & Sohn, 1991.

Austria—Economics

562. Arndt, Sven W., ed. *The Political Economy of Austria.* AEI Symposia, 82D. Washington, D.C.: American Enterprise Institute for Public Policy Research, 1982.

563. Knotzinger, Helmut, and Walter Koneczny. *Aspects of Economics and Taxation in Austria.* Extended and updated new ed. Vienna: Service Fachverlag an der Wirtschaftsuniversität, 1989.

Austria—European Community Relations

564. European Economic Community. *Agreement Between the European Economic Community and the Republic of Austria: With Final Act and Exchange of Letters, Brussels, 22 July 1972.* London: H.M.S.O., 1972.

Austria—Foreign Relations

565. Bauer, Robert A., ed. *The Austrian Solution—International Conflict and Cooperation.* Charlottesville: Published for the Johns Hopkins Foreign Policy Institute. School of Advanced International Studies, the Johns Hopkins University by the University Press of Virginia, 1982.

566. Cronin, Audrey Kurth. *Great Power Politics and the Struggle over Austria, 1945–1955.* Cornell Studies in Security Affairs. Ithaca: Cornell University Press, 1986.

567. McGovern, George Stanley. *Perspectives on Détente—Austria, Romania, and Czechslovakia: A Report to the Committee on Foreign Relations, United States Senate.* Washington, D.C.: G.P.O., 1979.

568. Schlesinger, Thomas O. *Austrian Neutrality in Postwar Europe.* Vienna; Stuttgart: W. Braumuller, 1972.

Austria—History

569. Bader, William B. *Austria Between East and West, 1945–1955.* Stanford: Stanford University Press, 1966.

570. Kreissler, Felix. *La prise de conscience de la nation autrichienne: 1938–1945–1978.* Publications de l'Université de Rouen. 2 vols. Paris: Presses universitaires de France, 1980.

571. Mokotoff, Gary, and Sallyann Amdur Sack. *Where Once We Walked: A Guide to Jewish Communities Destroyed in the Holocaust.* Teaneck, N.J.: Avotaynu, 1991.

572. Pauley, Bruce F. *From Prejudice to Persecution: A History of Austrian Anti-Semitism.* Chapel Hill: University of North Carolina Press, 1992.

573. Whitnah, Donald Robert, and Edgar L. Erickson. *The American Occupation of Austria.* Contributions in Military Studies, no. 46. Westport, Conn.: Greenwood Press, 1985.

Austria—Literature

574. Best, Alan D., and Hans Wolfschutz, eds. *Modern Austrian Writing: Literature and Society after 1945.* London: Oswald Wolff; and Totowa, N.J.: Barnes & Noble, 1980.

575. Cernyak-Spatz, Susan E., and Charles S. Merrill, eds. *Language and Culture: A Transcending Bond: Essays and Memoirs by American Germanists of Austro-Jewish Descent.* New York: Lang, 1993.

576. Daviau, Donald G., ed. *Major Figures of Contemporary Austrian Literature.* New York: P. Lang, 1987.

577. Demetz, Peter. *After the Fires: Recent Writing in the Germanies, Austria, and Switzerland.* 1st Harvest/HBJ ed. San Diego: Harcourt Brace Jovanovich, 1992.

578. Opel, Adolf, ed. *Anthology of Modern Austrian Literature.* London: Oswald Wolff, 1981.

Austria—Minorities

579. Barker, Thomas Mack, and Andreas Moritsch. *The Slovene Minority of Carinthia.* 2d ed. East Central European Studies. New York: Columbia University Press, 1979.

580. Turk, Danilo, ed. *Twenty Years Overdue: Slovene and Croat Minorities in Austria.* Translated by Bozidar Pahor and Albina Luk. Ljubljana: Institute for Ethnic Problems, 1976.

581. Wistrich, Robert S, ed. *Austrians and Jews in the Twentieth Century.* New York: St. Martin's Press, 1992.

Austria—Music

582. Brody, Elaine, and Claire Brook. *The Music Guide to Austria and Germany.* New York: Dodd Mead, 1975.

583. Smith, Joan Allen. *Schoenberg and His Circle.* New York: Schirmer Books; and London: Collier Macmillan, 1986.

584. Weiner, Marc A. *Undertones of Insurrection: Music, Politics, and the Social Sphere in the Modern German Narrative.* Texts and Contexts, no. 6. Lincoln: University of Nebraska Press, 1993.

Austria—Politics and Government

585. Bluhm, William Theodore. *Building an Austrian Nation: The Political Integration of a Western State.* New Haven: Yale University Press, 1973.

586. Fitzmaurice, John. *Austrian Politics and Society Today: In Defence of Austria.* New York: St. Martin's Press, 1990.

587. Houska, Joseph J. *Influencing Mass Political Behavior: Elites and Political Subcultures in the Netherlands and Austria.* Research Series, no. 60. Berkeley: Institute of International Studies, University of California, Berkeley, 1985.

588. Mitten, Richard. *The Politics of Antisemitic Prejudice: The Waldheim Phenomenon in Austria.* Boulder: Westview Press, 1992.

589. Riedlsperger, Max E. *The Lingering Shadow of Nazism: The Austrian Independent Party Movement Since 1945.* East European Monographs, no. 42. Boulder: East European Quarterly, 1978.

590. Sully, Melanie A. *Political Parties and Elections in Austria.* New York: St. Martin's Press, 1981.

BELGIUM

Belgium—Art

591. Collard, Jacques. *50 artistes de Belgique.* L'Art pour tous, no. 1. Bruxelles: Viva Press, 1984.

592. Langui, Emile. *Expressionism in Belgium*. Translated by Alistair Kennedy. Belgium, Art of Our Time. Brussels: Laconti, 1972.

Belgium—Colonialism

593. Grimal, Henri. *Decolonization: The British, Dutch, and Belgian Empires, 1919–1963*. Translated by Stepan De Vos. London: Routledge & Kegan Paul, 1978.

594. Vandewoude, Emile. *Liste de documents divers relatifs à l'expansion belge d'outre-mer, 1825–1961*. Bruxelles: Archives Générales du Royaume, 1982.

Belgium—Economics

595. Baudhuin, Fernand. *Histoire économique de la Belgique: 1957–1968*. Bruxelles: E. Bruylant, 1970.

596. Belgium. Ministry of Economic Affairs. *Belgium's Economy: Facts and Figures*. Brussels: The Ministry, 1985.

597. Brabander, Guido L. de. *Regional Specialization, Employment, and Economic Growth in Belgium from 1846 to 1970*. Dissertations in European Economic History. New York: Arno Press, 1981.

598. Desmit, Bart. *Les consequences économiques de l'abolition de l'association monetaire belgo-luxembourgeoise*. Genève: Institut universitaire de hautes études internationales, 1989.

599. Mommen, André. *The Belgian Economy in the Twentieth Century*. Contemporary Economic History of Europe Series. London and New York: Routledge, 1994.

Belgium—European Community Relations

600. Meerhaeghe, Marcel Alfons Gilbert van, ed. *Belgium and EC Membership Evaluated*. EC Membership Evaluated Series. London: Pinter Publishers; and New York: St. Martin's Press, 1992.

Belgium—Foreign Relations

601. Belgium. Ministère des affaires étrangères, du commerce exterieur et de la cooperation au développement. *Belgium's Policy in Africa*. Memo From Belgium, no. 194. Brussels: The Ministry, 1984.

602. Depoele, L. van. *Belgian-American Relations Concerning the Origin of the North Atlantic Treaty, 1948–1949*. Brussels: Center for American Studies, 1976.

603. Helmreich, Jonathan E. *Belgium and Europe: A Study in Small Power Diplomacy*. Issues in Contemporary Politics, Historical and Theoretical Perspectives, no. 3. The Hague: Mouton, 1976.

604. Kieft, David Owen. *Belgium's Return to Neutrality: An Essay in the Frustrations of Small Power Diplomacy*. Oxford: Clarendon Press, 1972.

605. Odom, Thomas Paul. *Shaba II: The French and Belgian Intervention in Zaire in 1978*. Fort Leavenworth, Kan.: U.S. Army Command and General Staff College, Combat Studies Institute, 1993.

606. Raeymaeker, Omer de. *Belgium and the Israeli-Arab Conflicts, 1948–1982*. Memo From Belgium, no. 192. Brussels: Ministry of Foreign Affairs, External Trade, and Cooperation in Development, 1984.

Belgium—Geography

607. Denis, Jacques, Modest Goossens, and A. Pissart, eds. *Geography in Belgium*. Namur: Comité national de géographie, 1984.

608. Murphy, Alexander B. *The Regional Dynamics of Language Differentiation in Belgium: A Study in Cultural-Political Geography*. Geography Research Paper, no. 227. Chicago: University of Chicago, Committee on Geographical Studies, 1988.

Belgium—History

609. Gerard, Jo. *Chronique de la Regence, 1944–1950*. Collection "Presence du passé." Bruxelles: J.M. Collet, 1983.

610. Haegendoren, Maurits van. *The Flemish movement in Belgium*. Antwerp: Flemish Cultural Council, 1965.

611. Lijphart, Arend, ed. *Conflict and Coexistence in Belgium: The Dynamics of a Culturally Divided Society*. Research Series, no. 46. Berkeley: Institute of International Studies, University of California, 1981.

612. Stephany, Pierre. *Nos années cinquante: Une histoire de l'après-guerre*. Document Duculot. Paris: Duculot, 1987.

613. Warmbrunn, Werner. *The German Occupation of Belgium, 1940–1944*. American University Studies. Series IX, History, no. 122. New York: P. Lang, 1993.

Belgium—Immigration

614. Gaudier, Jean-Pierre, and Philippe Hermans, ed. *Des Belges marocains: Parler à l'immigré, parler de l'immigré.* L'Homme, l'étranger. Bruxelles: De Boeck Université, 1991.

615. Leman, Johan. *From Challenging Culture to Challenged Culture: The Sicilian Cultural Code and the Socio-Cultural Praxis of Sicilian Immigrants in Belgium.* Studia anthropologica. Leuven: Leuven University Press, 1987.

616. Targosz, Patricia, ed. *L'Immigration et la recherche en Belgique, 1930–1991: Bilan.* SYBIDI document, no. 7. Louvain-la-Neuve: Academia: SYBIDI, 1993.

Belgium—Language

617. Willemart, Hélène, Pierre Willemart, and Sus van Elzen. *La Belgique et ses populations.* Pays et populations, no. 12. Bruxelles: Complexe, 1980.

Belgium—Literature

618. *Appel au jour: Poèmes et récits d'écrivains néerlandais et français de Belgique, recueillis dans le cadre de la campagne contre les assasinats politiques.* Cahier (Leuvense Schrijversaktie), nr. 38. Leuven: Leuvense Schrijversaktie, en collaboration avec Amnesty International Belgium, 1983.

619. Hanse, Joseph. *Naissance d'une littérature.* Archives du futur. Bruxelles: Editions Labor, 1992.

620. *Lettres belges de langue française: Lettres belges de langue néerlandaise.* Bruxelles: Europalia 80, 1980.

621. Mallinson, Vernon. *Modern Belgian Literature, 1830–1960.* New York: Barnes & Noble, 1966.

Belgian—Music

622. Beuvens, Guy, ed. *Guide de la musique de la communauté française de Belgique.* Bruxelles: Conseil de la musique de la communauté française de Belgique: Crédit communal, 1986.

623. Brody, Elaine, and Claire Brook. *The Music Guide to Belgium, Luxembourg, Holland, and Switzerland.* New York: Dodd, Mead, 1977.

624. Hen, Ferdinand J. de. *Music in Belgium.* Memo From Belgium, no. 186. Brussels: Ministry of Foreign Affairs, External Trade and Cooperation in Development, 1979.

Belgium—Politics and Government

625. Fitzmaurice, John. *The Politics of Belgium: Crisis and Compromise in a Plural Society.* 2d ed. London: C. Hurst, 1988.

626. Gijsels, Hugo. *Le Barbares: Les immigrés et le racisme dans la politique belge.* Berchem: EPO, 1988.

627. Gijsels, Hugo, and Jos vander Velpen. *Le chagrin des Flamands: Le Vlaams Blok de 1938 à nos jours.* Bruxelles: EPO, 1992.

628. Kitschelt, Herbert, and Staf Hellemans. *Beyond the European Left: Ideology and Political Action in the Belgian Ecology Parties.* Durham: Duke University Press, 1990.

629. Senelle, Robert. *The Political, Economic and Social Structures of Belgium.* Memo from Belgium, nos. 122–124. Brussels: Ministry of Foreign Affairs and External Trade, 1970.

630. Spaak, Paul-Henri. *The Continuing Battle: Memoirs of a European, 1936–1966.* Translated by Henry Fox. Boston: Little, Brown, 1971. Originally published as: *Combats inachevés.*

Belgium—Religion

631. Dascotte, Robert. *Religion et traditions populaires dans la région du Centre.* Maine-Saint-Paul, Belgium: R. Dascotte, 1982.

632. Voye, Liliane. *Sociologie du geste religieux: De l'analyse de la pratique dominicale en Belgique à une interpretation théorique.* Questions économiques, sociales et politiques. Bruxelles: Vie Ouvrière, 1973.

BRITAIN

Britain—Art

633. Compton, Susan, ed. *British Art in the 20th Century.* Munich: Prestel-Verlag, 1986.

634. Gilpin, George H. *The Art of Contemporary English Culture.* New York: St. Martin's Press, 1991.

635. Parry-Crooke, Charlotte, ed. *Contemporary British Artists.* London: Bugstrom & Boyle Books, 1979.

636. Spalding, Frances, and Judith Collins, eds. *20th Century Painters and Sculptors.* Woodbridge, Suffolk: Antique Collectors' Club, 1990.

637. Windsor, Alan, ed. *Handbook of Modern British Painting, 1900–1980*. Aldershot, Hampshire, and Brookfield, Vt.: Scolar Press, 1992.

British—Colonialism

638. Darwin, John. *The End of the British Empire: The Historical Debate*. Making Contemporary Britain. Oxford and Cambridge, Mass.: Blackwell, 1991.

639. Howe, Stephen. *Anticolonialism in British Politics: The Left and the End of Empire, 1918–1964*. Oxford Historical Monographs. Oxford: Clarendon Press; and New York: Oxford University Press, 1993.

640. Louis, William Roger. *Imperialism at Bay: The United States and the Decolonization of the British Empire, 1941–1945*. New York: Oxford University Press, 1978.

641. Low, Donald Anthony. *Eclipse of Empire*. Cambridge and New York: Cambridge University Press, 1991.

Britain—Economics

642. Burnham, Peter. *The Political Economy of Postwar Reconstruction*. Houndmills, Basingstoke: Macmillan, 1990.

643. Cairncross, Alec. *The British Economy Since 1945*. Making Contemporary Britain. Oxford and Cambridge, Mass.: Blackwell, 1992.

644. Cloke, Paul, ed. *Policy and Change in Thatcher's Britain*. Policy Planning and Critical Theory. New York: Pergamon Press, 1992.

645. Gamble, Andrew, and S. A. Walkland. *The British Party System and Economic Policy, 1945–1983*. Oxford: Clarendon Press; and New York: Oxford University Press, 1984.

646. Lowe, Rodney. *The Welfare State in Britain Since 1945*. New York: St. Martin's Press, 1993.

Britain—Ethnicity and Immigration

647. Alderman, Geoffrey. *Modern British Jewry*. Oxford: Clarendon Press; and New York: Oxford University Press, 1992.

648. Aurora, Gurdip Singh. *The New Frontiersmen; A Sociological Study of Indian Immigrants in the United Kingdom*. Bombay: Popular Prakashan, 1967.

649. Bhat, Ashok, Roy A. Carr-Hill, and Sushel Ohri, eds. *Britain's Black Population: A New Perspective*. 2d ed. Aldershot, Hampshire, and Brookfield, Vt.: Glower, 1988.

650. Booth, Heather. *The Migration Process in Britain and West Germany: Two Demographic Studies of Migrant Populations.* Research in Ethnic Relations Series. Aldershot, Hampshire, and Brookfield, Vt.: Avebury, 1992.

651. Brock, Colin, ed. *The Caribbean in Europe: Aspects of the West Indian Experience in Britain, France, and the Netherlands.* London and Totowa, N.J.: F. Cass, 1986.

652. Cashmore, Ellis, and Eugene McLaughlin, eds. *Out of Order?: Policing Black People.* London and New York: Routledge, 1991.

653. Cross, Malcom, and Han Entzinger, eds. *Lost Illusions: Caribbean Minorities in Britain and the Netherlands.* London: Routledge, 1988.

654. Daye, Sharon J. *Middle-Class Blacks in Britain: A Racial Fraction of a Class Group or a Class Fraction of a Racial Group?* New York: St. Martin's Press, 1994.

655. Ellis, June, ed. *West African Families in Britain: A Meeting of Two Cultures.* Library of Social Work. London and Boston: Routledge and K. Paul, 1978.

656. Kalara, Surajita Singha. *Daughters of Tradition: Adolescent Sikh Girls and Their Accommodation to Life in British Society.* Birmingham: Third World Publications, 1980.

657. Layton-Henry, Zig. *The Politics of Immigration: Immigration, "Race" and "Race" Relations in Post-War Britain.* Making Contemporary Britain. Oxford and Cambridge, Mass.: Blackwell, 1992.

658. Lester, Anthony, and Geoffrey Bindman. *Race and Law in Great Britain.* London: Longman, 1972.

659. Peach, Ceri. *West Indian Migration to Britain: A Social Geography.* London and New York: Published for the Institute of Race Relations by Oxford University Press, 1968.

660. Solomos, John. *Race and Racism in Britain.* 2d ed. New York: St. Martin's Press, 1993.

Britain—European Community Relations

661. Bulmer, Simon, Stephen George, and Andrew Scott, eds. *The United Kingdom and EC Membership Evaluated.* EC Membership Evaluated Series. New York: St. Martin's Press, 1992.

662. George, Stephen, ed. *Britain and the European Community: The Politics of Semi-Detachment.* Oxford: Clarendon Press; and New York: Oxford University Press, 1992.

663. Greenwood, Sean. *Britain and European Cooperation Since 1945.* Historical Association Studies. Oxford; and Cambridge, Mass.: Blackwell, 1992.

664. Lord, Christopher. *British Entry to the European Community Under the Heath Government of 1970–4.* Aldershot, Hampshire, and Brookfield, Vt.: Dartmouth, 1993.

665. Westlake, Martin. *Britain's Emerging Euro-Elite: The British in the Directly Elected European Parliament.* Adlershot, Hants, and Brookfield, Vt.: Dartmouth, 1994.

Britain—Foreign Relations

666. Aldrich, Richard James, ed. *British Intelligence, Strategy, and the Cold War, 1945–51.* London and New York: Routledge, 1992.

667. Byrd, Peter, ed. *British Foreign Policy Under Thatcher.* Oxford: P. Allen; and New York: St. Martin's Press, 1988.

668. Sanders, David. *Losing an Empire, Finding a Role: An Introduction to British Foreign Policy Since 1945.* Houndmills, Basingstoke: Macmillan, 1990.

669. Tugendhat, Christopher. *Options for British Foreign Policy in the 1990s.* Chatham House Papers. New York: Published in North America for the Royal Institute of International Affairs by Council on Foreign Relations Press, 1988.

670. Young, John W., ed. *The Foreign Policy of Churchill's Peacetime Administration, 1951–1955.* Leicester: Leicester University Press, 1988.

Britain—Geography

671. Beaver, Stanley Henry, A. D. M. Phillips, and Brian John Turton, eds. *Environment, Man and Economic Change.* London and New York: Longman, 1975.

672. Champion, Anthony Gerard, and Alan R. Townsend. *Contemporary Britain: A Geographic Perspective.* London and New York: E. Arnold, 1990.

673. Tolson, A. R., and M. E. Johnstone. *A Geography of Britain.* 3d ed. London: Oxford University Press, 1976.

Britain—History

674. Bartlett, Christopher John. *A History of Postwar Britain, 1945–1974.* London and New York: Longman, 1977.

675. Catterall, Peter. *British History: 1945–1987: An Annotated Bibliography*. Oxford and Cambridge, Mass.: Blackwell, 1991.

676. Cook, Chris, and David Waller. *The St. Martin's Guide to Sources in Contemporary British History*. Vol. 1. New York: St. Martin's Press, 1993.

677. Havinghurst, Alfred F. *Britain in Transition: The Twentieth Century*. 4th ed. Chicago: University of Chicago Press, 1985.

678. Morgan, Kenneth O. *The People's Peace: British History, 1945–1990*. Oxford and New York: Oxford University Press, 1992.

679. Pearce, Malcolm, and Geoffrey Stewart. *British Political History, 1867–1990: Democracy and Decline*. London and New York: Routledge, 1992.

680. Porter, Bernard. *The Lion's Share: A Short History of British Imperalism, 1850–1983*. 2d ed. London and New York: Longman, 1984.

681. Robbins, Keith. *The Eclipse of a Great Power: Modern Britain, 1870–1992*. 2d ed. Foundations of Modern Britain. London and New York: Longman, 1994.

682. Robbins, Keith. *History, Religion, and Identity in Modern Britain*. London and Rio Grande, Ohio: Hambledon Press, 1993.

Britain—Language

683. Grillo, R. D. *Dominant Languages: Languages and Hierarchy in Britain and France*. Cambridge and New York: Cambridge University Press, 1989.

684. Lockwood, William Burley. *Languages of the British Isles Past and Present*. The Language Library. London: A. Deutsch, 1975.

685. Price, Glanville. *The Languages of Britain*. London and New York: E. Arnold, 1984.

686. Rampton, Ben. *Crossing: Language and Ethnicity Among Adolescents*. Real Language Series. London and New York: Longman, 1995.

687. Stedman, Carolyn, Cathy Urwin, and Valerie Walkerdine, eds. *Language, Gender, and Childhood*. London and Boston: Routledge & Kegan Paul, 1985.

688. Sutcliffe, David M., and Ansel Wong, eds. *The Language of the Black Experience: Cultural Expression Through Word and Sound in the Caribbean and Black Britain*. Oxford and New York: Blackwell, 1986.

Britain—Literature

689. Ashcroft, Bill, Gareth Griffiths, and Helen Tiffin. *The Empire Writes Back: Theory and Practice in Post-Colonial Literatures.* New Accents. London and New York: Routledge, 1989.

690. Bloom, Harold, ed. Twentieth-Century British Literature. *The Chelsea House Library of Literary Criticism.* 6 vols. New York: Chelsea House Publishers, 1985–1987.

691. Brown, Dennis. *The Poetry of Post Modernity: Anglo/American Encodings.* New York: St. Martin's Press, 1994.

692. Dabydeen, David, and Nana Wilson-Tagoe. *A Reader's Guide to West Indian and Black British Literature.* A Hansib Educational Book. London: Rutherford, 1988.

693. Duncker, Patricia. *Sisters and Strangers: An Introduction to Contemporary Feminist Fiction.* Oxford and Cambridge, Mass.: Blackwell, 1992.

694. Gervais, David. *Literary Englands: Versions of "Englishness" in Modern Writing.* Cambridge and New York: Cambridge University Press, 1993.

695. Grewal, Shabnam, ed. *Charting the Journey. Writings by Black and Third World Women.* London: Sheba Feminist Publishers, 1988.

696. Kenner, Hugh. *A Sinking Island: The Modern English Writers.* New York: Knopf, 1988. Reprint. Baltimore: Johns Hopkins University Press, 1989.

697. *Location Register of Twentieth-Century English Literary Manuscripts and Letters: A Union List of Papers of Modern English, Irish, Scottish, and Welsh Authors in the British Isles.* 2 vols. Boston: G. K. Hall, 1988.

698. Morrison, Blake. *The Movement: English Poetry and Fiction of the 1950s.* Oxford and New York: Oxford University Press, 1980.

699. Ngcogo, Lauretta, ed. *Let It Be Told: Essays by Black Women in Britain.* London: Virago, 1988.

700. Sinfield, Alan. *Literature, Politics, and Culture in Postwar Britian.* The New Historicism, no. 12. Berkeley: University of California Press, 1989.

701. Swinden, Patrick. *The English Novel of History and Society, 1940–80.* New York: St. Martin's Press, 1984.

702. Watson, George. *British Literature Since 1945.* New York: St. Martin's Press, 1991.

Britain—Music

703. Foreman, Lewis, ed. *British Music Now: A Guide to the Work of Younger Composers.* London: P. Elek, 1975.

704. Griffiths, Paul. *New Sounds, New Personalities: British Composers of the 1980s.* London and Boston: Faber Music Ltd. in Association with Faber and Faber, 1985.

705. Leach, Gerald. *British Composer Profiles.* 2d ed. High Beeches, Gerrards Cross: British Music Society, 1989.

706. Oliver, Paul, ed. *Black Music in Britain: Essays on the Afro-Asian Contribution to Popular Music.* Popular Music in Britain. Milton Keynes, U.K. and Philadelphia: Open University Press, 1990.

707. Routh, Francis. *Contemporary British Music: the Twenty-Five Years from 1945 to 1970.* London: MacDonald and Co., 1972.

Britain—Politics and Government

708. Anderson, Bruce. *John Major: The Making of the Prime Minister.* London: Fourth Estate, 1991.

709. Birch, Anthony Harold. *The British System of Government.* 9th ed. London and New York: Routledge, 1993.

710. Brand, Jack. *British Parliamentary Parties.* Oxford: Clarendon Press; and New York: Oxford University Press, 1992.

711. Gamble, Andrew M., and S. A. Walkland. *The British Party System and Economic Policy, 1945–1983.* Oxford: Clarendon Press; and New York: Oxford University Press, 1984.

712. Holme, Richard, and Michael Elliott, eds. *Time for a New Constitution: 1688–1988.* Houndmills, Basingstoke: Macmillan, 1990.

713. Jefferys, Kevin. *The Labour Party Since 1945.* New York: St. Martin's Press, 1993.

714. Mount, Ferdinand. *The British Constitution Now: Recovery or Decline?* London: Heinemann, 1992.

715. Part, Anthony. *The Making of a Mandarin.* London: A. Deutsch, 1990.

716. Saggar, Shamit. *Race and Politics in Britain.* Contemporary Political Studies. New York and London: Harvester Wheatsheaf, 1992.

717. Sampson, Anthony. *The Essential Anatomy of Britain: Democracy in Crisis.* San Diego: Harcourt Brace, 1993.

718. Savage, Stephen P., and Lynton J. Robins, eds. *Public Policy Under Thatcher*. New York: St. Martin's Press, 1990.

719. Stevenson, John. *Third Party Politics Since 1945: the Politics of the Centre in Britain*. Oxford and Cambridge, Mass.: Blackwell, 1993.

Britain—Religion

720. Cesarani, David. *The Jewish Chronicle and Anglo-Jewry, 1841–1991*. Cambridge and New York: Cambridge University Press, 1994.

721. Gerloff, Roswith, I. H. *A Plea for British Black Theologies*. 3 vols. Frankfurt am Main and New York: P. Lang, 1992.

722. Hornsby-Smith, Michael P. *Roman Catholic Beliefs in England*. Cambridge and New York: Cambridge University Press, 1991.

723. Iqbal, Muhammad, Dharam Kumar Vohra, and Arjan Kirpal Singh. *East Meets West: A Background to Some Asian Faiths*. 3d ed., rev. London: Commission for Racial Equality, 1981.

724. Joly, Daniele. *Making a Place for Islam in British Society: Muslims in Birmingham*. Research Papers in Ethnic Relations, no. 4. Coventry: Centre for Research in Ethnic Relations, 1987.

725. Norman, Edward R. *Church and Society in England, 1770–1970*. Oxford: Clarendon Press, 1976.

CYPRUS

Cyprus—Economics

726. Wilson, Rodney. *Cyprus and the International Economy*. New York: St. Martin's Press, 1992.

Cyprus—Foreign Relations

727. Koumoulides, John. T. A., ed. *Greece and Cyprus in History*. Amsterdam: A.M. Hakkert, 1985.

728. Stern, Laurence Marcus. *The Wrong Horse: The Politics of Intervention and the Failure of American Diplomacy*. New York: Time Books, 1977.

729. United States. Congress. Senate. Committee on Foreign Relations. *New Opportunities for U.S. Policy in the Eastern Mediterranean: A Staff Report to the Committee on Foreign Relations*. Washington, D.C.: G.P.O., 1989.

Cyprus—Geography

730. Karouzes, Giorgos, and Andreas Sophocleous. *Cyprus Geographic Bibliography.* Nicosia: Cyprus Geological Association, 1972.

Cyprus—History

731. Cyprus. Grapheío Typou kai Plérophoríon. *The Refugees of Cyprus.* Nicosia: Press and Information Office, Republic of Cyprus, 1992.

732. Mayes, Stanley. *Cyprus and Makarios.* London: Putnam, 1960.

733. Salem, Norma, ed. *Cyprus, a Regional Conflict and its Resolution.* New York: St. Martin's Press in association with the Canadian Institute for International Peace and Security, Ottawa, 1992.

Cyprus—Literature

734. Dekavalles, Antones, ed. *The Voice of Cyprus: An Anthology of Cypriot Literature.* New York: October House, 1966.

735. Sophocleous, Andreas, ed. *Five Short Essays on Cypriot Literature.* Translated by John Vickers and Lana der Parthogh. Nicosia: Cyprus PEN, 1981.

Cyprus—Migration

736. Anthias, Floya. *Ethnicity, Class, Gender, and Migration: Greek-Cypriots in Britain.* Research in Ethnic Relations Series. Aldershot, Hampshire, and Brookfield, Vt.: Avebury, 1992.

737. Bhatti, F. M. *Turkish Cypriots in London.* Research Papers, no. 11. Birmingham: Center for the Study of Islam and Christian-Muslim Relations, 1981.

Cyprus—Politics and Government

738. Adams, Thomas W., and Alvin J. Cottrell. *Cyprus Between East and West.* Studies in International Affairs, no. 7. Baltimore: Johns Hopkins Press, 1968.

739. Arnold, Percy. *Cyprus Challenge.* London: Hogarth Press, 1956.

740. Battle, Lucius D., Dennis P. Williams, and Taylor G. Belcher. *Cyprus, Two Decades of Crisis.* Middle East Problem Paper, no. 16. Washington: Middle East Institute, 1978.

741. Xydis, Stephen George. *Cyprus, Reluctant Republic.* Near and Middle East Monographs, no. 11. The Hague: Mouton, 1973.

DENMARK

Denmark—Economics

742. Johansen, Hans Christian. *The Danish Economy in the Twentieth Century*. Croom Helm Series on the Contemporary Economic History of Europe. London: Croom Helm, 1987.

743. Miller, Kenneth E. *Denmark, a Troubled Welfare State*. Westview Profiles. Nations of Contemporary Western Europe. Boulder: Westview Press, 1991.

744. Nannestad, Peter. *Danish Design or British Disease?: Danish Economic Crisis Policy, 1974–1979*. Acta Jutlandica, 67:2. Social Science Series, no. 20. Aarhus, Denmark: Aarhus University Press, 1991.

Denmark—Ethnic Relations

745. Goldberger, Leo, ed. *The Rescue of the Danish Jews: Moral Courage Under Stress*. New York: New York University Press, 1987.

746. Kongelige Bibliotek. *Kings and Citizens: The History of the Jews in Denmark 1622–1983*. 2 vols. New York: Jewish Museum, 1983.

Denmark—European Community Relations

747. Thomsen, Birgit Nuchel, ed. *The Odd Man Out?: Danmark og den Europaiske integration 1948–1992*. Odense University Studies in History and Social Sciences, no. 169. Odense: Odense University Press, 1993.

Denmark—Fine Arts

748. Boesen, Gudmund. *Danish Museums*. Copenhagen: Committee for Danish Cultural Activities Abroad, 1966.

749. Skriver, Poul Erik, and Gunhild Starcke, eds. *Guide to Modern Danish Architecture*. Copenhagen: Arkitektens forlag, 1964.

Denmark—Foreign Relations

750. Haagerup, Niels Jorgen. *A Brief Introduction to Danish Foreign Policy and Defence*. 2d ed. Copenhagen: Information and Welfare Service of the Danish Defence, 1980.

751. Holbraad, Carsten. *Danish Neutrality*. Oxford: Clarendon Press and New York: Oxford University Press, 1991.

752. Holtermann, Henrik. *Danish Foreign Policy: Literature in Languages Other Than Danish, 1979–1986*. Copenhagen: Danish Institute of International Studies: Association of Danish Lawyers and Economists, 1988.

753. Seymour, Susan. *Anglo-Danish Relations and Germany, 1933–1945*. Odense University Studies in History and Social Sciences, no. 78. Odense: Odense University Press, 1982.

Denmark—History

754. Oakley, Stewart P. *A Short History of Denmark*. New York: Praeger, 1972.

755. Petrow, Richard. *The Bitter Years: The Invasion and Occupation of Denmark and Norway, April 1940–May 1945*. New York: Morrow, 1974.

Denmark—Language

756. Davidsen-Nielsen, Niels. *Tense and Mood in English: A Comparison with Danish*. Topics in English Linguistics, 1. Berlin and New York: Mouton de Gruyter, 1990.

757. Norlev, Erling, and Hans Anton Koefoed. *The Way to Danish*. 3d ed. Copenhagen: Munksgaard, 1968.

Denmark—Literature

758. Claudi, Jorgen. *Contemporary Danish authors*. Copenhagen: Danske Selskab, 1952.

759. Jorgensen, Aage. *Contributions in Foreign Languages to Danish Literary History, 1961–1981: A Bibliography*. Ballerup, Denmark: Bibliotekscentralen, 1982.

760. Kristensen, Sven. *Contemporary Danish Literature*. Danish Reference Papers. Copenhagen: Danske Selskab, 1956.

761. Mitchell, Phillip Marshall. *A History of Danish Literature*. 2d ed. New York: Kraus-Thomson, 1971.

Denmark—Music

762. Kappel, Vagn. *Contemporary Danish Composers Against the Background of Danish Musical Life and History*. 3d ed. Danes of the Past and Present. Copenhagen: Danske Selskab, 1967.

Denmark—Politics and Government

763. Denmark. Medicinaldirektorens sekretariat. *Public Administration and Health Care in Denmark.* Copenhagen: National Board of Health of Denmark, 1984.

764. Einhorn, Eric S. *National Security and Domestic Politics in Post-War Denmark.* Odense University Studies in History and Social Sciences, no. 27. Odense: Odense University Press, 1975.

765. Sjøblom, Gunnar. *The Roles of Political Parties in Denmark and in Sweden, 1970–84.* Forskningsrapport, 1985/6. Copenhagen: Institute of Political Studies, University of Copenhagen, 1985.

FINLAND

Finland—Art and Architecture

766. Poole, Scott. *The New Finnish Architecture.* New York: Rizzoli, 1992.

767. Seminar on Architecture and Urban Planning in Finland (1982: Helsinki, Finland). *Genius loci: A Search for Local Identity.* Helsinki: SAFA, 1982.

768. Smith, John Boulton. *Modern Finnish Painting and Graphic Art.* London: Weidenfeld & Nicolson, 1970.

Finland—Economics

769. Finland. Valtioneuvosto. *Sustainable Development and Finland.* Helsinki: Finnish Govt. Printing Center, 1991.

Finland—Foreign Relations

770. Leppanen, Seppo, ed. *The Soviet Union, Eastern Europe, and Finland.* VATT-Discussion Papers; no. 8. Helsinki: Govt. Institute for Economic Research, 1991.

771. Maude, George. *The Finnish Dilemma: Neutrality in the Shadow of Power.* London and New York: Published for the Royal Institute of International Affairs by Oxford University Press, 1976.

772. Wuorinen, John Henry, ed. *Finland and World War II, 1939–1944.* New York: Ronald Press, 1948. Reprint. Westport, Conn.: Greenwood Press, 1983.

Finland—Geography

773. Hautamäki, Lauri, Olli Kultalahti, and Seppo Siirila. *Approaches to Regional Development.* Research Reports. Series B; 37/1985. Tampere: Dept. of Regional Studies, University of Tampere, 1985.

774. Platt, Raye Roberts. *Finland and Its Geography.* An American Geographical Society Handbook. New York: Duell, Sloan and Pearce, 1955.

Finland—History

775. Engman, Max, and D. G. Kirby, eds. *Finland: People, Nation, State.* London: C. Hurst & Co.; and Bloomington: Indiana University Press, 1989.

776. Finland. National Archives. *Guide to the Public Archives of Finland.* Helsinki: The Archives, 1980.

777. Singleton, Frederick Bernard. *A Short History of Finland.* Cambridge and New York: Cambridge University Press, 1989.

Finland—Language

778. Chesterman, Andrew. *On Definiteness: A Study with Special Reference to English and Finnish.* Cambridge Studies in Linguistics; no. 56. Cambridge and New York: Cambridge University Press, 1991.

779. Sulkala, Helena, and Merja Karjalainen. *Finnish.* Descriptive Grammars. London and New York: Routledge, 1992.

780. Vahamëki, K. Borje. *Existence and Identity: A Study of the Semantics and Syntax of Existential Sentences in Finnish.* Meddelanden frän Stiftelsens för Abo akademi forskningsinstitut, nr. 99. Abo: Abo akademi, 1984.

781. Vilkuna, Maria. *Free Word Order in Finnish.* Suomalaisen Kirjallisuuden Seuran Toimituksia, nr. 500. Helsinki: Suomalaisen Kirjallisuuden Seura, 1989.

Finland—Literature

782. Ahokas, Jaakko. *A History of Finnish Literature.* Bloomington: Published for the American-Scandinavian Foundation by Indiana University, Research Center for the Language Sciences, 1973.

783. Andersen, Frank Egholm, and John M. Weinstock, eds. *The Nordic Mind: Current Trends in Scandinavian Literary Criticism.* Lanham, Md.: University Press of America, 1986.

784. Laitinen, Kai. *Literature of Finland: An Outline*. Helsinki: Otava, 1985.

785. Rubulis, Aleksis. *Baltic Literature: A Survey of Finnish, Estonian, Latvian, and Lithuanian Literatures*. Notre Dame: University of Notre Dame Press, 1970.

Finland—Music

786. Aarnio, Inkeri, Kauko Karjalainen, and Valdemar Melanko, eds. *Music of Finland*. Translated by Andrew Bentley, William Moore, and the English Center, Helsinki. Helsinki: Finnish Music Information Centre, 1983.

787. De Gorog, Lisa S., and Ralph De Gorog. *From Sibelius to Sallinen*. Contributions to the Study of Music and Dance; no. 16. New York: Greenwood Press, 1989.

788. Hodgson, Antony. *Scandinavian Music: Finland & Sweden*. Rutherford: Fairleigh Dickinson University Press; and London; Cranbury, N.J.: Associated University Presses, 1984.

Finland—Politics and Government

789. Arter, David. *Politics and Policy-Making in Finland*. Brighton, Sussex: Wheatsheaf Books; and New York: St. Martin's Press, 1987.

790. Mylly, Juhani, and R. Michael Berry, eds. *Political Parties in Finland*. Political History; no. C:21. Turku, Finland: Dept. of Political History, University of Turku, 1984.

FRANCE

France—Art

791. Ameline, Jean-Paul. *Les Nouveaux Realistes*. Jalons. Paris: Centre Georges Pompidou, 1992.

792. Bernier, Rosamond. *Matisse, Picasso, Miro, As I Knew Them*. New York: Knopf, 1991.

793. Ceysson, Bernard. *Vingt-cinq ans d'art en France, 1960–1985*. Paris: Larousse, 1986.

794. Guilbaut, Serge. *Reconstructing Modernism: Art in New York, Paris, and Montreal, 1945–1964*. Cambridge: MIT Press, 1990.

795. Inventaire général des monuments et des richesses artistiques de la France. *Répertoire des inventaires*. Paris: Impr. nationale, 1970.

796. Inventaire général des monuments et des richesses artistiques de la France. *Répertoire des photogrammes d'architecture de l'Inventaire*. Paris: Ministère de la culture, Direction du patrimoine, Inventaire général des monuments et des richesses artistiques de la France, 1984.

797. Millet, Catherine. *L'Art Contemporaine en France*. Paris: Flammarion, 1987.

798. Moulin, Raymonde, and Pascaline Costa. *L'Artiste, l'institution, et le marché*. Serie Art, histoire, société. Paris: Flammarion, 1992.

799. Simon, Matila. *The Battle of the Louvre: the Struggle to Save French Art in World War II*. New York: Hawthorn Books, 1971.

France — Colonialism

800. Aldrich, Robert. *France and the South Pacific Since 1940*. Honolulu: University of Hawaii Press, 1993.

801. Clayton, Anthony. *The Wars of French Decolonization*. Modern Wars in Perspective. London and New York: Longman, 1994.

802. Fanon, Frantz. *The Damned*. Foreword by Jean-Paul Sartre. Translated by Constance Farrington. Paris: Présence Africaine, 1963. Originally published as Les Damnés de la terre.

803. Fanon, Frantz. *Toward the African Revolution: Political Essays*. Translated by Haakon Chevalier. New Evergreen ed. New York: Grove Press, 1988. Originally published as *Pour la révolution africaine*.

804. Harrison, Christopher. *France and Islam in West Africa, 1860–1960*. African Study Series, no. 60. Cambridge and New York: Cambridge University Press, 1988.

805. Kent, John. *The Internationalization of Colonialism: Britain, France, and Black Africa, 1939–1956*. Oxford Studies in African Affairs. Oxford: Clarendon Press; and New York: Oxford University Press, 1992.

806. Osborne, Michael A. *Nature, the Exotic, and the Science of French Colonialism*. Science, Technology, and Society. Bloomington: Indiana University Press, 1994.

807. Smith, Tony. *The French Stake in Algeria 1945–1962*. Ithaca, N.Y.: Cornell University Press, 1978.

808. Westfall, Gloria. *French Colonial Africa: A Guide to Official Sources*. London and New York: Hans Zell Publishers, 1992.

France—Economics

809. Boyer, Robert. *The Regulation School: A Critical Introduction.* Translated by Craig Charney. New York: Columbia University Press, 1990. Originally published as *Théorie de la régulation.*

810. Kuisel, Richard F. *Capitalism and the State in Modern France: Renovation and Economic Management in the Twentieth Century.* Cambridge and New York: Cambridge University Press, 1981.

811. Scott, Bruce R., and Audrey T. Sproat. *National Industrial Planning—France and the EEC.* Boston: Division of Research, Harvard Business School, 1983.

812. Sutton, Michael. *France to 2000: the Challenge of a Changing Europe.* EIU Economic Prospects Series. London and New York: Economist Intelligence Unit, 1992.

France—European Community Relations

813. Auquier, Antoine A. *French Industry's Reaction to the European Common Market.* Outstanding Dissertations in Economics. New York: Garland, 1984.

814. Bergsten, Eric. *Community Law in the French Courts: The Law of Treaties in Modern Attire.* The Hague: M. Nijhoff, 1973.

815. Delors, Jacques. *Our Europe: The Community and National Development.* Translated by Brian Pearce. London and New York: Verso, 1992. Originally published as *La France par L'Europe.*

816. Dreyfus, François G., Jacques Morizet, and Max Peyrard, eds. *France and EC Membership Evaluated.* EC Membership Evaluated Series. London: Pinter Publishers; and New York: St. Martin's Press, 1993.

817. Muth, Hanns Peter. *French Agriculture and the Political Integration of Western Europe.* European Aspects. Series C: Politics no. 22. Leiden: Sijthoff, 1970.

818. Poidevin, Raymond. *Robert Schuman.* Politiques & Chretiens, no. 4. Paris: Beauchesne, 1988.

819. Sutton, Michael. *France to 2000: The Challenge of a Changing Europe.* EIU Economic Prospects Series. London and New York: Economist Intelligence Unit, 1992.

France—Foreign Relations

820. Bourgi, Robert. *Le Général de Gaulle et l'Afrique noire: 1940–1969*. Bibliothèque africaine et malgache: Droit, sociologie politique et économie, no. 33. Paris: Librairie générale de droit et de jurisprudence, 1980.

821. Friend, Julius Weis. *The Linchpin: French-German Relations, 1950–1990*. The Washington Papers, no. 154. New York: Praeger, 1991.

822. Lequesne, Christian. *Paris-Bruxelles: Comment se fait la politique européenne de la France*. Paris: Presses de la Fondation nationale des sciences politiques, 1993.

823. McCarthy, Patrick, ed. *France-Germany, 1983–1993: The Struggle to Cooperate*. New York: St. Martin's Press, 1993.

824. Saint-Prot, Charles. *La France et le renouveau arabe: De Charles de Gaulle à Valery Giscard d'Estaing*. Paris: Copernic, 1980.

825. Serfaty, Simon. *France, De Gaulle, and Europe: The Policy of the Fourth and Fifth Republics Toward the Continent*. Baltimore: Johns Hopkins Press, 1968.

826. Young, John W. *France, the Cold War, and the Western Alliance, 1944–1949.: French Foreign Policy and Post-War Europe*. New York: St. Martin's Press, 1990.

France—Geography and Regional Planning

827. Huss, Marie Monique. *Demography, Public Opinion, and Politics in France, 1974–80*. London: Dept. of Geography, Queen Mary College, University of London, 1980.

828. Pinchemel, Philippe. *France: A Geographical Survey*. Translated by Christine Trollope and Arthur J. Hunt. London: Bell, 1969. Originally published as *Géographie de la France*.

829. Thompson, Ian Bentley. *The Paris Basin*. 2d ed. Oxford and New York: Oxford University Press, 1981.

France—History

830. Beevor, Antony, and Artemis Cooper. *Paris After the Liberation*. New York: Doubleday, 1994.

831. Carrard, Philippe. *Poetics of the New History: French Historical Discourse from Braudel to Chartier*. Parallax. Baltimore: Johns Hopkins University Press, 1992.

832. Duchen, Claire. *Women's Rights and Women's Lives in France, 1944–1968*. London and New York: Routledge, 1994.

833. Flanner, Janet. *Paris Journal, 1944–65*. London: Gollancz, 1966.

834. Guillaume, Sylvie. *La France Contemporaine, 1946–1990: Chronologie Commentée*. 2 vols. Paris: Perrin, 1990–1991.

835. Hemmendinger, Judith. *Survivors: Children of the Holocaust*. Foreword by Elie Wiesel. Zenith ed. Bethesda, Md.: National Press, 1986. Originally published as *Enfants de Buchenwald*.

836. Hughes, Henry Stuart. *The Obstructed Path: French Social Thought in the Years of Desperation, 1930–1960*. New York: Harper and Row, 1968.

837. Judt, Tony. *Past Imperfect: French Intellectuals, 1944–1956*. Berkeley: University of California Press, 1992.

838. Mendras, Henri, and Alistair Cole. *Social Change in Modern France: Towards a Cultural Anthropology of the Fifth Republic*. Cambridge and New York: Cambridge University Press; and Paris: Editions de la Maison de Sciences de l'Homme, 1991. Originally published as *La second révolution française*.

839. Moxon-Browne, Edward. *Terrorism in France*. Conflict Studies, no. 144. London: Institute for the Study of Conflict, 1983.

840. Northcutt, Wayne, ed. *Historical Dictionary of the French Fourth and Fifth Republics, 1946–1991*. Historical Dictionaries of French History. New York: Greenwood Press, 1992.

841. Rioux, Jean-Pierre. *The Fourth Republic, 1944–1958*. Translated by Godfrey Rogers. The Cambridge History of Modern France; no. 7. Cambridge and New York: Cambridge University Press; and Paris: Editions de la Maison des Sciences de l'Homme, 1987. Originally published as *La France de la Quatrième République*.

842. Rohan, Marc. *Paris '68: graffiti, posters, newspapers, and poems of the events of May 1968*. London: Impact Books, 1988.

843. Ross, George, Stanley Hoffmann, and Sylvia Malzacher, eds. *The Mitterrand Experiment: Continuity and Change in Modern France*. New York: Oxford University Press, 1987.

844. Rubenstein, Diane. *What's Left?: The Ecole Normale Supérieure and the Right*. Rhetoric of the Human Sciences. Madison: University of Wisconsin Press, 1990.

845. Spender, Stephen. *European Witness*. New York: Reynal and Hitchcock, 1946.

846. Todd, Emmanuel. *The Making of Modern France: Ideology, Politics, and Culture*. Translated by Anthony and Betty Forster. Oxford and Cambridge, Mass.: Blackwell, 1991.

France—Immigration

847. Bousquet, Gisele Luce. *Behind the Bamboo Hedge: The Impact of Homeland Politics in the Parisian Vietnamese Community*. Ann Arbor: University of Michigan Press, 1991.

848. Boyarin, Jonathan. *Polish Jews in Paris: the Ethnography of Memory*. The Modern Jewish Experience. Bloomington: Indiana University Press, 1991.

849. Brock, Colin, ed. *The Caribbean in Europe: Aspects of the West Indian Experience in Britain, France, and the Netherlands*. London and Totowa, N.J.: F. Cass, 1986.

850. Cross, Gary S. *Immigrant Workers in Industrial France: the Making of a New Laboring Class*. Philadelphia: Temple University Press, 1983.

851. Grillo, R. D. *Ideologies and Institutions in Urban France: The Representation of Immigrants*. Cambridge and New York: Cambridge University Press, 1985.

852. *Guide actuel du Paris mondial: Paris afro-antillais, Paris arabe, Paris asiatique, Paris de l'Est, Paris juif, Paris latino*. Paris: Seuil, 1992.

853. Silverman, Maxim. *Deconstructing the Nation: Immigration, Racism, and Citizenship in Modern France*. Critical Studies in Racism and Migration. London and New York: Routledge, 1992.

854. Silverman, Maxim, ed. *Race, Discourse, and Power in France*. Research in Ethnic Relations Series. Aldershot, Hampshire, Avebury; and Brookfield, Vt.: Gower, 1991.

855. Stein, Louis. *Beyond Death and Exile: the Spanish Republicans in France, 1939–1955*. Cambridge: Harvard University Press, 1979.

France—Language

856. Ager, D. E. *Sociolinguistics and Contemporary French*. Cambridge and New York: Cambridge University Press, 1990.

857. Grau, Richard. *Les langues et les cultures minoritaires en France: Une approche juridique contemporaine.* Documentation du Conseil de la langue française, no. 18. Québec: Conseil de la langue française, 1985.

858. Grau, Richard. *Le statut juridique de la langue française en France.* Documentation du Conseil de la langue française, no. 8. Québec: Conseil de la langue française, 1981.

859. Pope, Mildred Katharine. *From Latin to Modern French.* 2d rev. ed. Manchester, U.K.: Manchester University Press, 1952.

860. Rickard, Peter. *A History of the French Language.* 2d ed. London; Boston: Unwin Hyman, 1989.

861. Sellers, Susan. *Language and Sexual Difference: Feminist Writing in France.* New York: St. Martin's Press, 1991.

862. Vassberg, Lilliane Mangold. *Alsatian Acts of Identity: Language Use and Language Attitudes in Alsace.* Multilingual Matters, no. 90. Clevedon, U.K. and Philadelphia: Multilingual Matters, 1993.

863. Vermes, Geneviève, ed. *Vingt-cinq communautés linguistiques de la France.* 2 vols. Paris: L'Harmattan, 1988.

France—Literature

864. Boon, James A. *From Symbolism to Structuralism: Levi-Strauss in a Literary Tradition.* Explorations of Interpretive Sociology. New York: Harper & Row, 1972.

865. Bree, Germaine. *Twentieth Century French Literature.* Translated by Louise Guiney. Chicago: University of Chicago Press, 1983.

866. Burnier, Michel Antoine. *Choice of Action: the French Existentialists on the Political Front Line.* Translated by Bernard Murchland. 1st American ed. New York: Random House, 1968. Originally published as *Les existentialistes et la politique.*

867. Champagne, Roland A. *French Structuralism.* Twayne's World Authors Series, no. 818. Boston: Twayne Publishers, 1990.

868. Doubrovsky, Serge. *The New Criticism in France.* Translated by Derek Coltman. Chicago: University of Chicago Press, 1973. Originally published as *Pourquoi la nouvelle critique.*

869. Haft, Cynthia J. *The Theme of Nazi Concentration Camps in French Literature.* New Babylon: Studies in the Behavioral Sciences, no. 12. The Hague: Mouton, 1973.

870. Hargreaves, Alec G. *Voices From the North African Immigrant Community in France.* Berg French Studies Series. New York: Berg, 1991.

871. Harris, Frederick John. *Encounters with Darkness: French and German Writers on World War II.* New York: Oxford University Press, 1983.

872. Hollier, Denis, and R. Howard Bloch, eds. *A New History of French Literature.* Cambridge: Harvard University Press, 1989.

873. Jardine, Alice A., and Anne M. Menke, eds. *Shifting Scenes: Interviews on Women, Writing, and Politics in Post-68 France.* Gender and Culture. New York: Columbia University Press, 1991.

874. Lechte, John. *Julia Kristeva.* London and New York: Routledge, 1990.

875. Sartre, Jean-Paul. *What Is Literature?* Translated by Bernard Frechtman. London: Methuen, 1967. Originally published as *Qu'est-ce que la littérature?*

876. Suleiman, Susan Rubin. *Subversive Intent: Gender, Politics, and the Avant-Garde.* Cambridge: Harvard University Press, 1990.

France—Music

877. Myers, Rollo H. *Modern French Music: Its Evolution and Cultural Background From 1900 to the Present Day.* Oxford: Blackwell, 1971.

878. Nectoux, Jean-Michel. *The New Grove Twentieth-Century French Masters: Faure, Debussy, Satie, Ravel, Poulenc, Messiaen, Boulez.* 1st American ed. New York: Norton, 1986.

France—Politics and Government

879. Bedarida, François, and Michael Pollak, eds. *Mai 68 et les sciences sociales.* Cahiers de l'Institut d'histoire du temps present, no. 11. Paris: L'Institut, 1989.

880. Cole, Alistair, ed. *French Political Parties in Transition.* Aldershot, Hampshire, and Brookfield, Vt.: Dartmouth, 1990.

881. Duverger, Maurice. *The French Political System.* Chicago: University of Chicago Press, 1958.

882. Frears, John R. *Parties and Voters in France.* London: Hurst; and New York: St. Martin's Press, 1991.

883. Giles, Frank. *The Locust Years: The Story of the Fourth French Republic, 1946–1958.* New York: Carroll & Graf, 1994.

884. Hanley, David L., A. P. Kerr, and Neville H. Waites. *Contemporary France: Politics and Society Since 1945.* New ed. London and New York: Routledge, 1989.

885. Keeler, John T. S. *The Politics of Neocorporatism in France: Farmers, the State, and Agricultural Policy-Making in the Fifth Republic.* New York: Oxford University Press, 1987.

886. Pickles, Dorothy. *Problems of Contemporary French Politics.* London and New York: Methuen, 1982.

887. Shennan, Andrew. *Rethinking France: Plans for Renewal, 1940–1946.* Oxford: Clarendon Press; and New York: Oxford University Press, 1989.

France—Religion

888. Etienne, Bruno, ed. *L'Islam en France.* Collection "Etudes de l'Annuaire de l'Afrique du Nord." Paris: Editions du Centre National de la Recherche Scientifique, 1990.

889. Kepel, Gilles. *Les banlieues de l'Islam. Naissance d'une religion en France.* L'Epreuve des faits. Paris: Seuil, 1987.

890. Ravitch, Norman. *The Catholic Church and the French Nation, 1589–1989.* London and New York: Routledge, 1990.

891. Schnapper, Dominique. *Jewish Identities in France.* Translated by Arthur Goldhammer. Chicago: University of Chicago Press, 1983. Originally published as *Juifs et israélites.*

892. Université des Sciences Humaines de Strasbourg. Centre de Sociologie du Protestantisme. *Eglises et groupes religieux dans la société française.* Strasbourg: CERDIC Publications, 1977.

GERMANY

Germany—Colonialism

893. Crozier, Andrew J. *Appeasement and Germany's Last Bid for Colonies.* New York: St. Martin's Press, 1988.

894. Schmokel, Wolfe W. *Dream of Empire: German Colonialism, 1919–1945.* Yale Historical Publications: Miscellany, no. 78. Reprint. Westport, Conn.: Greenwood Press, 1980.

895. Stoecker, Helmuth, ed. *German Imperialism in Africa. From the Beginnings Until the Second World War.* Translated by Bernd

Zollner. London: C. Hurst; and Atlantic Highlands, N.J.: Humanities Press International, 1986. Originally published as *Drang nach Afrika*.

Germany—Cultural Life

896. Jarausch, Konrad Hugo. *The Unfree Professions: German Lawyers, Teachers, and Engineers, 1900–1950*. New York: Oxford University Press, 1990.

897. Nicholas, Lynn H. *The Rape of Europa: The Fate of Europe's Treasures in the Third Reich & the Second World War*. New York: Knopf, 1994.

898. Santner, Eric L. *Stranded Objects: Mourning, Memory and Film in Postwar Germany*. Ithaca, N.Y.: Cornell University Press, 1990.

899. Stieg, Margaret F. *Public Libraries in Nazi Germany*. Tuscaloosa: University of Alabama Press, 1992.

900. Weber, John Paul. *The German War Artists*. Columbia, S.C.: Cerberus Book Co., 1979.

Germany—Economics

901. Backer, John H. *Priming the German Economy: American Occupational Policies, 1945–1948*. Durham: Duke University Press, 1971.

Germany—Education

902. Phillips, David, ed. *German Universities After the Surrender: British Occupation Policy and the Control of Higher Education*. Oxford: University of Oxford. Dept. of Educational Studies, 1983.

903. Tent, James F. *Mission on the Rhine: Reeducation and Denazification in American-Occupied Germany*. Chicago: University of Chicago Press, 1982.

Germany—Foreign Relations

904. Hanrieder, Wolfram F. *Germany, America, Europe: Forty Years of German Foreign Policy*. New Haven: Yale University Press, 1989.

905. Laqueur, Walter. *Russia and Germany: A Century of Conflict*. Boston: Little, Brown, 1965.

906. McAdams, James A. *Germany Divided: From the Wall to Reunification*. Princeton Studies in International History and Politics. Princeton: Princeton University Press, 1993.

907. Plock, Ernest D. *East German-West German Relations and the Fall of the GDR.* Boulder: Westview Press, 1993.

908. Tilford, Roger, ed. *The Ostpolitik and Political Change in Germany.* Saxon House Studies. Farnborough, Hampshire, and Saxon House; Lexington, Mass.: Lexington Books, 1975.

Germany—Geography

909. Freeman, Michael J. *Atlas of Nazi Germany.* New York: Macmillan, 1987.

910. Hilgemann, Werner. *Atlas zur deutschen Zeitgeschichte, 1918–1968: Ende des Kaiserreichs 1918, Weimarer Republik 1919–1933, "Drittes Reich" 1933–1945, Deutschland unter den Besatzungsmächten 1945–1949, Bundesrepublik Deutschland und DDR 1949–1968.* München: Piper, 1984.

Germany—History

911. Clemens, Diane Shaver. *Yalta.* New York: Oxford University Press, 1970.

912. Deighton, Anne. *The Impossible Peace: Britain, the Division of Germany and the Origins of the Cold War.* Oxford: Clarendon Press; and New York: Oxford University Press, 1990.

913. Ermarth, Michael, ed. *America and the Shaping of German Society, 1945–1955.* Providence: Berg, 1993.

914. Feis, Herbert. *Between War and Peace: The Potsdam Conference.* Princeton: Princeton University Press, 1960.

915. Gellately, Robert. *The Gestapo and German Society: Enforcing Racial Policy, 1933–1945.* Oxford: Clarendon Press; and New York: Oxford University Press, 1990.

916. Hersch, Gisela. *A Bibliography of German Studies, 1945–1971.* Bloomington: Indiana University Press, 1972.

917. Malzahn, Manfred. *Germany, 1945–1949: A Sourcebook.* London and New York: Routledge, 1991.

918. Paul, Barbara Dotts. *The Germans After World War II: An English-Language Bibliography.* Boston: G. K. Hall, 1990.

919. Sharp, Tony. *The Wartime Alliance and the Zonal Division of Germany.* Oxford: Clarendon Press, 1975.

920. Shirer, William L. *The Rise and Fall of the Third Reich: A History of Nazi Germany*. New York: Fawcett Crest, 1992.

921. Thompson, Wayne C., and Susan L. Thompson. *Historical Dictionary of Germany*. European Historical Dictionaries, no. 4. Metuchen, N.J.: Scarecrow Press, 1994.

Germany—Language

922. Durrell, Martin. *Using German: A Guide to Contemporary Usage*. Cambridge and New York: Cambridge University Press, 1992.

923. Russ, Charles V. J. *The German Language Today: A Linguistic Introduction*. London and New York: Routledge, 1994.

924. Russ, Charles V. J., ed. *The Dialects of Modern German: A Linguistic Survey*. London: Routledge, 1990.

925. Stevenson, Patrick, ed. *The German Language and the Real World: Sociolinguistic, Cultural, and Pragmatic Perspectives on Contemporary German*. Forthcoming.

926. Townson, Michael. *Mother-Tongue and Fatherland: Language and Politics in German*. Manchester, U.K., and New York: Manchester University Press, 1992.

Germany—Literature

927. Caviola, Hugo. *In the Zone: Perception and Presentation of Space in German and American Postmodernism*. Basel and Boston: Birkhauser Verlag, 1991.

928. Cernyak-Spatz, Susan E. *German Holocaust Literature*. Rev. ed. American University Studies. Series I, Germanic Languages and Literatures, no. 29. New York: P. Lang, 1989.

929. Critchfield, Richard. *When Lucifer Cometh: The Autobiographical Discourse of Writers and Intellectuals Exiled During the Third Reich*. Literature and the Sciences of Man, no. 7. New York: P. Lang, 1994.

930. Grass, Günter. *On Writing and Politics, 1967–1983*. Translated by Ralph Manheim. Introduction by Salman Rushdie. San Diego: Harcourt Brace Jovanovich, 1985.

931. Humble, Malcolm, and Raymond Furness. *An Introduction to German Literature, 1871–1990*. New York: St. Martin's Press, 1993.

932. McGlathery, James M., ed. *Music and German Literature: Their Relationship Since the Middle Ages*. Studies in German Literature, Linguistics, and Culture, no. 66. Columbia, S.C.: Camden House, 1992.

933. Pape, Walter, ed. *1870/71–1989/90: German Unifications and the Change of Literary Discourse*. European Cultures, no. 1. Berlin and New York: W. de Gruyter, 1993.

934. Reschke, Claus, and Howard Pollack, eds. *German Literature and Music: An Aesthetic Fusion, 1890–1989*. Houston German Studies, no. 8. München: W. Fink, 1992.

935. Stern, Joseph Peter. *The Dear Purchase: A Theme in German Modernism*. Cambridge Studies in German. Cambridge and New York: Cambridge University Press, 1995.

936. Stern, Joseph Peter. *The Heart of Europe: Essays on Literature and Ideology*. Oxford and Cambridge, Mass.: Blackwell, 1992.

Germany—Music

937. Einstein, Alfred. *Alfred Einstein on Music: Selected Music Criticisms*. Contributions to the Study of Music and Dance, no. 21. New York: Greenwood Press, 1991.

938. Levi, Erik. *Music in the Third Reich*. New York: St. Martin's Press, 1994.

939. Meyer, Michael. *The Politics of Music in the Third Reich*. American University Studies. Series IX, History, no. 49. New York: P. Lang, 1991.

940. Spotts, Frederic. *Bayreuth: A History of the Wagner Festival*. New Haven: Yale University Press, 1994.

Germany—Nuremberg Trials

941. Conot, Robert E. *Justice at Nuremberg*. New York: Harper & Row, 1983.

942. Ginsburgs, George, and Vladimir Nikolaevich Kudriavtsev, eds. *The Nuremberg Trial and International Law*. Dordrecht and Boston: M. Nijhoff, 1990.

943. Smith, Bradley F., ed. *The American Road to Nuremberg: The Documentary Record, 1944–1945*. Stanford: Hoover Institution Press, 1982.

944. Taylor, Telford. *The Anatomy of the Nuremberg Trials: A Personal Memoir*. New York: Knopf, 1992.

945. *Trial of the Major War Criminals Before the International Military Tribunal*. Reprint of the 1947–49 ed. 42 vols. New York: AMS Press, 1971.

Germany—Politics and Government

946. *German Basic Handbook: ABC of German Administration and Public Services*. London: The Foreign Office, 1944.

947. Gimbel, John. *The American Occupation of Germany: Politics and the Military, 1945–1949*. Stanford: Stanford University Press, 1968.

948. Krisch, Henry. *German Politics under Soviet Occupation*. New York: Columbia University Press, 1974.

949. Merritt, Anna J., Richard L. Merritt, and Kathleen Kelly Rummel. *Politics, Economics, and Society in the Two Germanies, 1945–75: A Bibliography of English-Language Works*. Urbana: University of Illinois Press, 1978.

Germany (1990+)—Economics

950. Graf, William D., ed. *The Internationalization of the German Political Economy*. International Political Economy Series. New York: St. Martin's Press, 1992.

951. Heilemann, Ullrich, and Reimut Jochimsen. *Christmas in July?: The Political Economy of German Unification Reconsidered*. Brookings Occasional Papers. Washington, D.C.: Brookings Institution, 1993.

952. Lipschitz, Leslie, and Donogh McDonald, eds. *German Unification: Economic Issues*. Occasional Paper (International Monetary Fund); no. 75. Washington, D.C.: International Monetary Fund, 1990.

953. Smyser, W. R. *The Economy of United Germany*. New York: St. Martin's Press, 1992.

954. Thomsen, Horst. *Bibliographie zur deutschen Einigung*. Rev. ed. of: *Bibliographie zur deutsch-deutschen Wirtschafts-, Wahrungs- und Sozialunion*. 1. Aufl. 1990. Kieler Schnellbibliographien zu aktuellen Wirtschaftsthemen; Bd. 2. Kiel: Bibliothek des Instituts für Weltwirtschaft an der Universität Kiel, 1991.

Germany (1990+)—European Community Relations

955. European Parliament. Directorate General for Research. *The Impact of German Unification on the European Community*. Research and Documentation Papers. Working Document; no. 1. Luxembourg: Office for Official Publications of the European Communities, 1990.

956. Heisenberg, Wolfgang, ed. *German Unification in European Perspective.* London and Washington: Brassey's, 1991.

957. Lankowski, Carl F., ed. *Germany and the European Community: Beyond Hegemony and Containment?* New York: St. Martin's Press, 1993.

958. Lippert, Barbara. *German Unification and EC Integration.* Chatham House Papers. New York: Council on Foreign Relations Press, 1993.

959. Remmers, Thomas. *Europäische Gemeinschaften und Kompetenzverluste der deutschen Länder.* European University Studies. Series II, Law, no. 1286. Frankfurt am Main and New York: P. Lang, 1992.

960. Seidel, Barbara. *Die Einbindung der Bundesrepublik Deutschland in die Europäischen Gemeinschaften als Problem des Finanzausgleichs.* Finanzwissenschaftliche Schriften, Bd. 50. Frankfurt am Main and New York: P. Lang, 1992.

Germany (1990+)—Foreign Relations

961. Garton Ash, Timothy. *In Europe's Name: Germany and the Divided Continent.* New York: Random House, 1993.

962. Stares, Paul B., ed. *The New Germany and the New Europe.* Washington, D.C.: Brookings Institution, 1992.

963. Wallach, H. G. Peter, and Ronald A. Francisco. *United Germany.* Westport: Praeger, 1992.

964. Wettig, Gerhard. *The Soviet Union and German Unification.* Cologne: Berichte des Bundesinstituts für Ostwissenschaftliche und Internationale Studien, 1990.

Germany (1990+)—History

965. Buruma, Ian. *The Wages of Guilt: Memories of War in Germany and Japan.* New York: Farrar, Straus & Giroux, 1994.

966. Grosser, Dieter, ed. *German Unification.* German Historical Perspectives, no. 7. Oxford and Providence: Berg, 1992.

967. Jeffery, Charlie, and Peter Savigear. *German Federalism Today.* New York: St. Martin's Press, 1991.

968. Library of Congress. Congressional Research Service. *Legal Issues Relating to the Future Status of Germany.* Washington, D.C.: G.P.O., 1990.

969. Schneider, Peter. *The German Comedy: Scenes of Life After the Wall.* Translated by Philip Boehm and Leigh Hafrey. New York: Farrar, Straus & Giroux, 1991. Originally published as *Extreme Mittellage.*

970. Turner, Henry Ashby. *Germany From Partition to Reunification.* Rev. ed. of: *The Two Germanies Since 1945.* New Haven: Yale University Press, 1992.

Germany (1990+)—Literature

971. Berman, Russell A. *Cultural Studies of Modern Germany: History, Representation, and Nationhood.* Madison: University of Wisconsin Press, 1993.

972. Eigler, Friederike, and Peter Pfeiffer, eds. *Cultural Transformations in the New Germany: American and German Perspectives.* Studies in German Literature, Linguistics, and Culture. Columbia, S.C.: Camden House, 1993.

Germany (1990+)—Politics

973. Asmus, Ronald D. *German Unification and Its Ramifications.* Santa Monica: RAND, 1991.

974. Coleman, William E., Jr., and William E. Coleman, Sr. *A Rhetoric of the People: The German Greens and the New Politics.* Westport: Praeger, 1993.

975. Conradt, David P. *The German Polity.* 5th ed. New York: Longman, 1993.

976. Livingston, Robert Gerald, and Volkmar Sander, eds. *The Future of German Democracy.* With an essay "On Loss" by Günter Grass. New York: Continuum, 1993.

977. Padgett, Stephen. *Parties and Party Systems in the New Germany.* Aldershot, Hampshire, and Brookfield, Vt.: Dartmouth, 1993.

978. Veen, Hans-Joachim, Norbert Lepszy, and Peter Mnich. *The Republikaner Party in Germany: Right-Wing Menace or Protest Catchall?* The Washington Papers, no. 162. Westport, Conn.: Praeger, with the Center for Strategic and International Studies, Washington, D.C., 1993.

Germany (East)—Economics

979. Childs, David, Thomas A. Baylis, and Marilyn Rueschemeyer, eds. *East Germany in Comparative Perspective.* London and New York: Routledge, 1989.

980. Baylis, Thomas A. *The Technical Intelligentsia and the East German Elite*. Berkeley: University of California Press, 1974.

Germany (East)—European Community Relations

981. Knodt, Michele. *Unterordnung der EC—Integration der DDR unter den deutschen Einigungsprozess*. Frankfurt am Main: Haag & Herchen, 1992.

982. Schmidt, Klaus-Peter. *Die Europäische Gemeinschaft aus der Sicht der DDR (1957–1989)*. Hamburg: Kovac, 1991.

Germany (East)—Foreign Relations

983. McAdams, A. James. *East Germany and Detente*. Soviet and East European Studies. Cambridge and New York: Cambridge University Press, 1985.

984. Stent, Angela. *From Embargo to Ostpolitik*. Soviet and East European Studies. Cambridge and New York: Cambridge University Press, 1981.

Germany (East)—History

985. Bracher, Karl Dietrich. *The German Dictatorship: The Origins, Structure, and Effects of National Socialism*. New York: Praeger, 1970.

986. Childs, David, ed. *Honecker's Germany*. London: Allen and Unwin, 1985.

987. Heitzer, Heinz. *GDR, an Historical Outline*. Dresden: Zeit im Bild, 1981.

988. McCauley, Martin. *The German Democratic Republic Since 1945*. New York: St. Martin's Press, 1983.

989. Nettl, J. P. *The Eastern Zone and Soviet Policy in Germany, 1945–50*. London: Oxford University Press, 1951. Reprint. New York: Octagon Books, 1977.

990. Schneider, Eberhard. *The GDR: The History, Politics, Economy and Society of East Germany*. New York: St. Martin's Press, 1978.

Germany (East)—Literature

991. Fox, Thomas C. *Border Crossings: An Introduction to East German Prose*. Ann Arbor: University of Michican Press, 1993.

992. Gerber, Margy, and Judith Pouget. *Literature of the German Democratic Republic in English Translation: A Bibliography*. Lanham, Md.: University Press of America, 1984.

993. Kane, Martin, ed. *Socialism and the Literary Imagination: Essays on East German Writers*. New York: Berg, 1991.

994. Reid, James Henderson. *Writing Without Taboos: The New East German Literature*. New York: Berg, 1990.

Germany (East)—Politics and Government

995. Beyme, Klaus von, and Hartmut Zimmermann, eds. *Policymaking in the German Democratic Republic*. New York: St. Martin's Press, 1983.

996. Ludz, Peter Christian. *The Changing Party Elite in East Germany*. Cambridge: MIT Press, 1972.

997. McCauley, Martin. *The German Democratic Republic Since 1945*. New York: St. Martin's Press, 1983.

998. McCauley, Martin. *Marxism-Leninism in the German Democratic Republic: The Socialist Unity Party (SED)*. Studies in Russian and East European History. New York: Barnes & Noble, 1979.

999. Sontheimer, Kurt, and Wilhelm Bleek. *The Government and Politics of East Germany*. Translated by Ursula Price. London: Hutchinson, 1975. Originally published as *DDR; Politik, Gesellschaft, Wirtschaft*.

Germany (East)—Social Structure

1000. Edwards, G. E. *GDR Society and Social Institutions*. London: Macmillan, 1985.

1001. Krejčí, Jaroslav. *Social Structure in Divided Germany*. London: Croom Helm, 1976.

Germany (West)—European Community Relations

1002. Bulmer, Simon. *The Domestic Structure of European Community Policy-Making in West Germany*. Outstanding Theses From the London School of Economics and Political Science. New York: Garland, 1986.

1003. Bulmer, Simon, and William Paterson. *The Federal Republic of Germany and The European Community*. London and Boston: Allen & Unwin, 1987.

1004. Deutsch, Karl. *France, Germany and the Western Alliance: A Study in Elite Attitudes on European Integration and World Politics*. New York: Scribner, 1967.

1005. Schweitzer, Carl-Christoph, and Detlev Karsten, eds. *The Federal Republic of Germany and EC Membership Evaluated*. EC Membership Evaluted Series. New York: St. Martin's Press, 1990.

1006. Simonian, Haig. *The Privileged Partnership: Franco-German Relations in the European Community, 1969–1984*. Oxford: Clarendon Press; and New York: Oxford University Press, 1985.

1007. Willis, Roy. *France, Germany and the New Europe*. 2d ed. Stanford: Stanford University Press, 1968.

Germany (West)—Foreign Relations

1008. Chubin, Shahram, ed. *Germany and the Middle East: Patterns and Prospects*. New York: St. Martin's Press, 1992.

1009. Diefendorf, Jeffry M., Axel Frohn, and Hermann-Josef Rupieper, eds. *American Policy and the Reconstruction of West Germany, 1945–1955*. Publications of the German Historical Institute. Washington, D.C.: German Historical Institute; and Cambridge; New York: Cambridge University Press, 1993.

1010. Goldmann, Kjell. *Change and Stability in Foreign Policy: The Problems and Possibilities of Detente*. Princeton: Princeton University Press, 1988.

1011. Griffith, William E. *The Ostpolitik of the Federal Republic of Germany*. Studies in Communism, Revisionism, and Revolution, no. 24. Cambridge: MIT Press, 1978.

1012. Hanrieder, Wolfram F. *Germany, America, Europe: Forty Years of German Foreign Policy*. New Haven: Yale University Press, 1989.

1013. Myers, Kenneth A. *Ostpolitik and American Security Interests in Europe*. Washington, D.C.: Center for Strategic and International Studies, Georgetown University, 1972.

1014. Pfetsch, Frank R. *West Germany, Internal Structures and External Relations: Foreign Policy of the Federal Republic of Germany*. New York: Praeger, 1988. Revised translation of: *Die Aussenpolitik der Bundesrepublik, 1949–1980*.

1015. Pittman, Avril. *From Ostpolitik to Reunification: West German-Soviet Political Relations Since 1974*. Soviet and East European Studies, no. 85. Cambridge and New York: Cambridge University Press, 1992.

1016. Schwartz, Thomas Alan. *America's Germany: John J. McCloy and the Federal Republic of Germany*. Cambridge: Harvard University Press, 1991.

1017. Wolffsohn, Michael. *Eternal Guilt?: Forty Years of German-Jewish-Israeli Relations*. Translated by Douglas Bokovoy. New York: Columbia University Press, 1993. Originally published as: *Ewige Schuld?*

Germany (West)—History

1018. Balfour, Michael. *West Germany: A Contemporary History*. London: Croom Helm, 1982.

1019. Craig, Gordon Alexander. *The Germans*. New York: Putnam, 1982.

1020. Diefendorf, Jeffry M., Axel Frohn, and Hermann-Josef Rupieper, eds. *American Policy and the Reconstruction of West Germany, 1945–1955*. Publications of the German Historical Institute. Washington, D.C.: German Historical Institute, 1993.

Germany (West)—Immigration

1021. Martin, Philip L. *The Unfinished Story: Turkish Labour Migration to Western Europe: With Special Reference to the Federal Republic of Germany*. Geneva: ILO, 1991.

Germany (West)—Literature

1022. Bullivant, Keith, ed. *After the "Death of Literature": West German Writing in the 1970s*. Oxford and New York: Berg, 1989.

1023. Krueger, Merle Curtis. *Authors and the Opposition: West German Writers and the Social Democratic Party From 1945 to 1969*. Stuttgarter Arbeiten zur Germanistik, nr. 107. Stuttgart: Akademischer Verlag, 1982.

1024. Riemann, Wolfgang. *Über das Leben in Bitterland: Bibliographie zur türkischen Deutschland—Literatur und zur türkischen Literatur in Deutschland*. Wiesbaden: O. Harrassowitz, 1990.

1025. Veteto-Conrad, Marilya J. *Finding a Voice: Identity and the Works of German-Language Turkish Writers in the FRG and Berlin (West)*. American University Studies. Series III, Comparative Literature, no. 48. New York: P. Lang, 1993.

Germany (West)—Politics and Government

1026. Berger, Stephen D. *The Development of Legitimating Ideas: Intellectuals and Politicians in Post-War Western Germany*. Harvard Studies in Sociology. New York: Garland, 1991.

1027. Doring, Herbert, and Gordon R. Smith, eds. *Party Government and Political Culture in Western Germany*. New York: St. Martin's Press, 1982.

1028. Fisher, Stephen L. *The Minor Parties of the Federal Republic of Germany: Toward a Comparative Theory of Minor Parties.* The Hague: M. Nijhoff, 1974.

1029. Kolinsky, Eva. *Parties, Opposition, and Society in West Germany.* New York: St. Martin's Press, 1984.

1030. Livingston, Robert Gerald, ed. *West German Political Parties: CDU, CSU, FDP, SPD, the Greens.* German Issues, no. 4. Washington, D.C.: American Institute for Contemporary German Studies, Johns Hopkins University, 1986.

1031. Padgett, Stephen, and Tony Burkett. *Political Parties and Elections in West Germany: The Search for a New Stability.* London: C. Hurst; and New York: St. Martin's Press, 1986.

1032. Smith, Gordon R. *Democracy in Western Germany: Parties and Politics in the Federal Republic.* 3d ed. Aldershot, Hampshire, and Gower, 1986.

Germany (West)—Religion

1033. Mihciyazgan, Ursula. *Moscheen türkischer Muslime in Hamburg.* Hamburg: Behörde für Arbeit, Gesundheit und Soziales, 1990.

1034. Ruh, Ulrich. *Religion und Kirche in der Bundesrepublik Deutschland.* Materialien zur Landeskunde. München: Iudicium Verlag, 1990.

1035. Stern, Frank. *The Whitewashing of the Yellow Badge: Antisemitism and Philosemitism in Postwar Germany.* Translated by William Templer. Studies in Antisemitism. Oxford and New York: Published for the Vidal Sassoon International Center for the Study of Antisemitism, the Hebrew University of Jerusalem by Pergamon Press, 1992.

GIBRALTAR

Gibraltar—Economics

1036. Maxwell Stamp Associates. *Gibraltar, British or Spanish?: The Economic Prospects.* London: Wilton House Publications, 1976.

Gibraltar—Foreign Relations

1037. Calvar, Jorge, and Edward J. Gueritz. *Gibraltar, the Strategic Theatre* and *A British Response.* Spain: Instituto de Cuestiones Internacionales, 1980.

1038. Levie, Howard S. *The Status of Gibraltar*. A Westview Replica Edition. Boulder: Westview Press, 1983.

1039. Morris, D. S., and R. H. Haigh. *Britain, Spain, and Gibraltar, 1945–1990*. London and New York: Routledge, 1992.

Gibraltar — History

1040. Bradford, Ernle Dusgate Selby. *Gibraltar: The History of a Fortress*. 1st American ed. New York: Harcourt Brace Jovanovich, 1972.

1041. Doak, Claude. *Gibraltar*. Edgemont, Pa.: Chelsea House Publishers, 1986.

1042. Green, Muriel M. *A Gibraltar Bibliography*. London: University of London, Institute of Commonwealth Studies, 1980.

1043. Jackson, William Godfrey Fothergill. *The Rock of the Gibraltarians*. Rutherford: Farleigh Dickinson University Press, 1987.

1044. Shields, Graham J. *Gibraltar*. World Bibliographical Series, no. 87. Oxford and Santa Barbara: Clio Press, 1987.

Gibraltar — Language

1045. Kramer, Johannes. *English and Spanish in Gibraltar*. Hamburg: H. Buske, 1986.

GREECE

Greece — Art

1046. Heliopoulou-Ronkan, Dora. *Three Generations of Greek Women Artists: Figures, Forms, and Personal Myths*. Athens: Greek Ministry of Culture; and Washington, D.C.: National Museum of Women in the Arts, 1989.

1047. Institute of Contemporary Arts (London, England). *Eight Artists, Eight Attitudes, Eight Greeks*. London: Institute of Contemporary Arts, 1975.

1048. Livas, Haris. *Contemporary Greek Artists*. New York: Vantage Press, 1993.

Greece — Economics

1049. Georgiou, Vasillios F. *Greece and the Transnational Corporations: Dependent Economic Development and its Constraints on National Policy, 1965–1985*. Occasional Papers, no. 15. Sydney:

Transnational Corporations Research Project, University of Sydney, 1988.

1050. McDonald, Robert. *Greece in the 1990s: Taking its Place in Europe*. Special Report, no. 2099. London and New York: Economist Intelligence Unit, 1991.

Greece—European Community Relations

1051. European Parliament. *Greece's Accession to the European Community*. Luxembourg: European Parliament, Secretariat, Directorate General for Research and Documentation, 1982.

1052. *Greece, the European Economic Community, and a European Free Trade Area: Documents Relating to the Position of Greece in the Negotiations for a European Free Trade Area Within the O.E.E.C.* Athens: Ministries of Co-ordination and Foreign Affairs of the Royal Hellenic Gov., 1959.

1053. Kazakos, Panos V., and Panayotis C. Ioakimidis, eds. *Greece and EC Membership Evaluated*. EC Membership Evaluated Series. London: Pinter Publishers; New York: St. Martin's Press, 1994.

1054. Yannopoulos, George, ed . *Greece and the EEC: Integration and Convergence*. New York: St. Martin's Press, 1986.

Greece—Foreign Relations

1055. Aegean Foundation. *United States Foreign Policy Regarding Greece, Turkey, and Cyprus*. Washington, D.C.: American Hellenic Institute, 1989.

1056. Bakcheli, Tozun. *Greek-Turkish Relations Since 1955*. Westview Special Studies in International Relations. Boulder: Westview Press, 1990.

1057. Gianaris, Nicholas V. *Greece & Turkey: Economic and Geopolitical Perspectives*. New York: Praeger, 1988.

1058. United States. Congress. House. Committee on Foreign Affairs. Subcommittee on Europe. *Greece, Spain, and the Southern NATO Strategy: Hearings, Ninety-Second Congress, First Session*. Washington, D.C.: G.P.O., 1971.

Greece—History

1059. Clogg, Richard, ed. *Greece in the 1980s*. New York: St. Martin's Press, 1983.

1060. Forster, Edward Seymour. *A Short History of Modern Greece, 1821–1956*. 3d ed. London: Methuen, 1958. Reprint. Westport, Conn.: Greenwood Press, 1977.

1061. Iatrides, John O., ed. *Greece in the 1940s: A Nation in Crisis.* Modern Greek Studies Association Series, no. 4. Hanover: University Press of New England, 1981.

1062. Iatrides, John O., ed. *Greece in the 1940s: A Bibliographic Companion*. Modern Greek Studies Association Series, no. 5. Hanover: University Press of New England, 1981.

1063. Koumoulides, John T. A., ed. *Greece and Cyprus in History*. Amsterdam: A. M. Hakkert, 1985.

1064. Richter, Heinz A. *Greece and Cyprus Since 1920: Bibliography of Contemporary History*. Heidelberg: Wissenschaftlicher Verlag Nea Hellas, 1984.

1065. Sarafis, Marion, ed. *Greece, From Resistance to Civil War*. Nottingham: Spokesman, 1980.

1066. Vlavianos, Haris. *Greece, 1941–49: From Resistance to Civil War. The Strategy of the Greek Communist Party*. New York: St. Martin's Press, 1992.

Greece—Language

1067. Joseph, Brian D. *Morphology and Universals in Syntactic Change: Evidence From Medieval and Modern Greek*. Outstanding Dissertations in Linguistics. New York: Garland, 1990.

1068. Tsakirides, Evris. *Spoken Greek*. 2d ed. Ann Arbor: University of Michigan Press, 1992.

1069. Watts, Niki. *Colloquial Greek*. The Colloquial Series. London and New York: Routledge, 1994.

Greece—Literature

1070. Alexiou, Margaret, and Vassilis Lambropoulos, eds. *The Text and its Margins: Post-Structuralist Approaches to Twentieth-Century Greek Literature*. New York: Pella Publishing Co., 1985.

1071. Beaton, Roderick. *An Introduction to Modern Greek Literature*. Forthcoming.

1072. Keeley, Edmund, and Peter Bien, eds. *Modern Greek Writers: Solomos, Calvos, Matesis, Palamas, Cavafy, Kazantzakis, Seferis, Elytis*. Princeton Essays in European and Comparative Literature, no. 7. Princeton: Princeton University Press, 1972.

1073. Lambropoulos, Vassilis. *Literature as National Institution: Studies in the Politics of Modern Greek Criticism.* Princeton: Princeton University Press, 1988.

1074. Lorentzatos, Zesimos. *"The Lost Center" and Other Essays in Greek Poetry.* Translated by Kay Cicellis. Princeton Essays in Literature. Princeton: Princeton University Press, 1980.

1075. Philippides, Dia Mary L. *Census of Modern Greek Literature: Check-list of English-Language Sources Useful in the Study of Modern Greek Literature (1824–1987).* Modern Greek Studies Association Series, no. 7. New Haven: The Association, 1990.

Greece—Politics and Government

1076. Clogg, Richard, ed. *Greece, 1981–89: The Populist Decade.* New York: St. Martin's Press, 1993.

1077. Clogg, Richard, and George Yannopoulos, eds. *Greece Under Military Rule.* London: Secker & Warburg, 1972.

1078. Schwab, Peter, and George D. Frangos, eds. *Greece Under the Junta.* Interim History. New York: Facts on File, 1970.

Greece—Religion

1079. Argenti, Philip Pandely. *The Religious Minorities of Chios: Jews and Roman Catholics.* Cambridge: Cambridge University Press, 1970.

1080. Hart, Laurie Kain. *Time, Religion, and Social Experience in Rural Greece.* Lanham, Md.: Rowman & Littlefield, 1992.

1081. Stewart, Charles. *Demons and the Devil: Moral Imagination in Modern Greek Culture.* Princeton Modern Greek Studies. Princeton: Princeton University Press, 1991.

Greece—Social Life and Customs

1082. Cowan, Jane K. *Dance and the Body Politic in Northern Greece.* Princeton Modern Greek Studies. Princeton: Princeton University Press, 1990.

1083. Loizos, Peter, and Euthymios Papataxiarches, eds. *Contested Identities: Gender and Kinship in Modern Greece.* Princeton Modern Greek Studies. Princeton: Princeton University Press, 1991.

ICELAND

Iceland—Cultural Life

1084. Hill, Dennis Auburn. *Icelandic Libraries and Archives*. Madison: Dept. of Scandinavian Studies, University of Wisconsin-Madison, 1988.

1085. Weingand, Darlene E. *Connections—Literacy and Cultural Heritage: Lessons from Iceland*. Metuchen, N.J.: Scarecrow Press, 1992.

1086. Gisli Palsson. *Coastal Economies, Cultural Accounts: Human Ecology and Icelandic Discourse*. Manchester, U.K., and New York: Manchester University Press, 1991.

Iceland—Economics

1087. Gunnarsson, Gudmundur. *The Economic Growth in Iceland, 1910–1980: A Productivity Study*. Uppsala: S. Academiae Upsaliensis, 1990. Originally published as *Ekonomiska tillvaxten på Island, 1910–80*.

Iceland—European Community Relations

1088. European Economic Community. *Agreement Between the European Economic Community and the Republic of Iceland*. London: H.M.S.O., 1972.

Iceland—Foreign Relations

1089. Benedikt, Grondal. *Iceland, From Neutrality to NATO Membership*. Scandia Books; no. 11. Oslo: Universitetsforlaget, 1971.

1090. Hannes Jonsson. *Friends in Conflict: The Anglo-Icelandic Cod Wars and the Law of the Sea*. London: C. Hurst; and Hamden, Conn.: Archon Books, 1982.

1091. Icelandic Association for Western Co-Operation. *Iceland, NATO, and Security in the Norwegian Sea: A Report From a Conference in Reykjavik, Iceland, 12th-13th March, 1987*. Reykjavik: Icelandic Association for Western Co-Operation, 1987.

Iceland—Geography

1092. Malmstrom, Vincent Herschel. *A Regional Geography of Iceland*. Foreign Field Research Program. Washington, D.C.: National Academy of Sciences, National Research Council, 1958.

1093. Preusser, Hubertus. *The Landscapes of Iceland: Types and Regions*. The Hague: W. Junk, 1976.

Iceland—History

1094. Sigurdur A. Magnusson. *Northern Sphinx: Iceland and the Icelanders From the Settlement to the Present*. Montreal: McGill-Queen's University Press, 1977.

1095. Tomasson, Richard F. *Iceland, the First New Society*. Minneapolis: University of Minnesota Press, 1980.

Iceland—Religion

1096. Bjørnsson, Bjørn. *The Lutheran Doctrine of Marriage in Modern Icelandic Society*. Scandinavian University Books. Oslo: Universitetsforlaget, 1971.

Iceland—Sociology

1097. Einarsson, Ingimar. *Patterns of Societal Development in Iceland*. Acta Universitatis Upsaliensis. Studia sociologica Upsaliensia; no. 26. Uppsala: Uppsala University, 1987.

1098. Sigurjon Bjørnsson, Wolfgang Edelstein, and Kurt Kreppner. *Explorations in Social Inequality: Stratification Dynamics in Social and Individual Development in Iceland*. Berlin: Max-Planck-Inst. für Bildungsforschung, 1977.

IRELAND

Ireland—Art

1099. Butler, Patricia. *Three Hundred Years of Irish Watercolours and Drawings*. London: Weidenfeld and Nicolson, 1990.

1100. Knowles, Roderic, ed. *Contemporary Irish Art*. Dublin: Wolfhound Press; with the assistance of the Arts Council, 1982.

Ireland—Economics

1101. Foley, Anthony, and Michael Mulreany, eds. *The Single European Market and the Irish Economy*. Dublin: Institute of Public Administration, 1990.

1102. Kennedy, Kieran Anthony, Thomas Giblin, and Deirdre McHugh. *The Economic Development of Ireland in the Twentieth Century*. Contemporary Economic History of Europe Series. London and New York: Routledge, 1988.

1103. Sweeney, Paul. *The Politics of Public Enterprise and Privatisation*. Dublin: Tomar, 1990.

1104. Tansey, Paul. *Making the Irish Labour Market Work*. Business and Economics Research Series. Dublin: Gill and Macmillan, 1991.

Ireland—European Community Relations

1105. Aughey, Arthur, Paul Hainsworth, and Martin J. Trimble. *Northern Ireland in the European Community: An Economic and Political Analysis*. Belfast: Policy Research Institute, 1989.

1106. Foley, Anthony, and Michael Mulreany, eds. *The Single European Market and the Irish Economy*. Dublin: Institute of Public Administration, 1990.

1107. Hederman, Miriam. *The Road to Europe: Irish Attitudes, 1948–61*. Dublin: Institute of Public Administration, 1983.

1108. Keatinge, Patrick, ed. *Ireland and EC Membership Evaluated*. EC Membership Evaluated Series. New York: St. Martin's Press, 1991.

1109. O'Donnell, Rory, and Patrick Honohan. *Economic and Monetary Union*. Studies in European Union, no. 2. Dublin: Institute of European Affairs, 1991.

1110. Paisley, Sylvia E. *A Guide to EEC Law in Northern Ireland*. Belfast: Faculty of Law, Queen's University, 1986.

1111. Reid, Madeleine. *The Impact of Community Law on the Irish Constitution*. ICEL (Series), no. 13. Dublin: Irish Center for European Law, Trinity College, 1990.

1112. Sharp, Paul. *Irish Foreign Policy and the European Community: A Study of the Impact of Interdependence on the Foreign Policy of a Small State*. Aldershot, Hampshire, Dartmouth; and Brookfield, Vt.: Gower, 1990.

Ireland—Foreign Relations

1113. Dwyer, T. Ryle. *Irish Neutrality and the USA, 1939–47*. Dublin: Gill and Macmillan, 1977.

Ireland—Geography

1114. Freeman, Thomas Walter. *Ireland: A General and Regional Geography*. 4th ed. London: Methuen, 1972.

Ireland — History

1115. Bailey, Anthony. *Acts of Union: Reports on Ireland, 1973–79*. New York: Random House, 1980.

1116. Bell, J. Bowyer. *The Secret Army: The IRA, 1916–1979*. Cambridge: MIT Press, 1980.

1117. Bew, Paul, and Henry Patterson. *Sean Lemass and the Making of Modern Ireland, 1945–66*. Dublin: Gill and Macmillan, 1982.

1118. Coogan, Tim Pat. *The IRA: A History*. Niwot, Col.: R. Rinehart, 1993.

1119. Keogh, Dermot, and Michael H. Haltzel, eds. *Northern Ireland and the Politics of Reconciliation*. Woodrow Wilson Center Series. Washington, D.C. and Cambridge: Woodrow Wilson Center Press and Cambridge University Press, 1993.

1120. Lustick, Ian. *State-Building Failure in British Ireland and French Algeria*. Research Series, no. 63. Berkeley: Institute of International Studies, University of California, 1985.

1121. McCluskey, Conn. *Up Off Their Knees: A Commentary on the Civil Rights Movement in Northern Ireland*. Belfast: Conn McCluskey and Associates, 1989.

1122. O'Malley, Padraig. *Biting at the Grave: The Irish Hunger Strikes and the Politics of Despair*. Boston: Beacon Press, 1990.

1123. O'Malley, Padraig. *The Uncivil Wars: Ireland Today*. Boston: Beacon Press, 1990.

1124. Ranelagh, John O'Beirne. *A Short History of Ireland*. Cambridge and New York: Cambridge University Press, 1983.

1125. Smyth, Clifford. *Ian Paisley: Voice of Protestant Ulster*. Edinburgh: Scottish Academic, 1987.

Ireland — Language

1126. O'Siadhail, Micheal. *Modern Irish: Grammatical Structure and Dialectal Variation*. Cambridge Studies in Linguistics. Supplementary Volume. Cambridge and New York: Cambridge University Press, 1989.

1127. Todd, Loreto. *The Language of Irish Literature*. The Language of Literature. New York: St. Martin's Press, 1989.

1128. Tovey, Hilary. *Language Policy and Socioeconomic Development in Ireland*. Occasional Paper (Linguistics Institute of Ireland); no. 4. Dublin: Linguistics Institute of Ireland, 1978.

Ireland—Literature

1129. Cahalan, James M. *Modern Irish Literature and Culture: A Chronology*. New York: G. K. Hall, 1993.

1130. Deane, Seamus. *Celtic Revivals: Essays in Modern Irish Literature, 1880–1980*. Winston Salem: Wake Forest University Press, 1987.

1131. Deane, Seamus. *A Short History of Irish Literature*. London: Hutchinson; and Notre Dame: University of Notre Dame Press, 1986.

1132. Deane, Seamus, Andrew Carpenter, and Jonathan Williams, eds. *The Field Day Anthology of Irish Writing*. 3 vols. Lawrence Hill, Derry: Field Day Publications, 1991.

1133. Donoghue, Denis. *We Irish: Essays on Irish Literature and Society*. New York: Knopf, 1986.

1134. Ellis, Peter Berresford. *A Dictionary of Irish Mythology*. London: Constable, 1987. Reprint. New York: Oxford University Press, 1991.

1135. McCormack, W. J. *The Battle of the Books: Two Decades of Irish Cultural Debate*. Gigginstown, Mullingar, Co. Westmeath: Lilliput Press, 1986.

1136. O'Driscoll, Robert, ed. *Theatre and Nationalism in Twentieth-Century Ireland*. London: Oxford University Press, 1971.

1137. Trevor, William. *The Collected Stories*. New York: Penguin, 1992.

Ireland—Migration

1138. Kearney, Richard, ed. *Migrations: The Irish at Home & Abroad*. Dublin: Wolfhound Press, 1990.

1139. Walsh, Brendan M., Robert Charles Geary, and Joseph Gerard Hughes. *Religion and Demographic Behavior in Ireland. Migration Between Northern Ireland and the Republic of Ireland*. Dublin: Economic and Social Research Institute, 1970.

Ireland—Music

1140. Deale, Edgar M. *A Catalogue of Contemporary Irish Composers*. Dublin: Music Association of Ireland, 1968.

1141. Gillen, Gerard, and Harry White, eds. *Musicology in Ireland*. Irish Musical Studies; no. 1. Dublin: Irish Academic Press, 1990.

1142. Molloy, Dinah. *Find Your Music in Ireland.* 2d ed. Dublin: The Arts Council, 1979.

Ireland — Politics and Government

1143. Chubb, Basil. *The Government & Politics of Ireland.* The Politics of the Smaller European Democracies. Stanford: Stanford University Press, 1970.

1144. Dooney, Sean, and John O'Toole. *Irish Government Today.* Dublin: Gill and Macmillan, 1992.

1145. Praeger, Jeffrey. *Building Democracy in Ireland.* Cambridge and New York: Cambridge University Press, 1986.

Ireland — Religion

1146. Bruce, Steve. *God Save Ulster: The Religion and Politics of Paisleyism.* Oxford: Clarendon Press; and New York: Oxford University Press, 1986.

1147. Clarke, Desmond M. *Church and State.* Cork: Cork University Press, 1984.

1148. Fulton, John. *The Tragedy of Belief: Division, Politics, and Religion in Ireland.* Oxford: Clarendon Press; and New York: Oxford University Press, 1991.

1149. Gallagher, Eric, and Stanley Worrall. *Christians in Ulster, 1968–1980.* Oxford and New York: Oxford University Press, 1982.

1150. Murray, Dominic. *Worlds Apart: Segregated Schools in Northern Ireland.* Belfast: Appletree Press, 1985.

1151. Nelson, Sarah. *Ulster's Uncertain Defenders: Protestant Political, Paramilitary and Community Groups and the Northern Ireland Conflict.* Irish Studies. Belfast: Appletree Press; and Syracuse: Syracuse University Press, 1984.

1152. New Ulster Political Research Group. *Beyond the Religious Divide.* Belfast: Ulster Defence Association, 1979.

1153. Walsh, Brendan M. *Religion and Demographic Behaviour in Ireland.* Economic and Social Research Institute, Paper no. 55. Dublin: The Institute, 1970.

1154. Whyte, John. *Catholics in Western Democracies: A Study in Political Behaviour.* New York: St. Martin's Press, 1981.

1155. Whyte, John. *Church and State in Modern Ireland, 1923–1979.* 2d ed. Dublin: Gill and Macmillan; and Totowa, N.J.: Barnes & Noble, 1980.

ITALY

Italy—Art

1156. Clemente, Francesco. *Clemente.* Vintage Contemporary Artists. New York: Vintage Books, 1987.

1157. Clemente, Francesco. *Testa coda.* New York: Gagosian Gallery: Rizzoli, 1991.

1158. Fagiolo Dell'Arco, Maurizio. *Balla, the Futurist.* New York: Rizzoli, 1988.

1159. Grisi, Laura, and Germano Celant. *Laura Grisi: A Selection of Works with Notes by the Artist: Essay-Interview by Germano Celant.* Translated by Marguerite Shore. New York: Rizzoli, 1990.

1160. Jentsch, Ralph. *The Artist and the Book in Twentieth-Century Italy.* Turin: Umberto Allemandi, 1992.

Italy—Colonialism

1161. Rennell, Francis James Rennell Rodd. *British Military Administration of Occupied Territories in Africa During the Years 1941–1947.* Westport, Conn.: Greenwood Press, 1970.

1162. Rivlin, Benjamin. *The United Nations and the Italian Colonies.* United Nations Action; Case Histories, no. 1. New York: Carnegie Endowment for International Peace, 1950.

1163. Rossi, Gianluigi. *L'Africa italiana verso l'indipendenza, 1941–1949.* Università di Roma, Facoltà di scienze politiche, no. 33. Milano: Giuffre, 1980.

Italy—Economics

1164. Bianchi, Carluccio, and Carlo Casarosa, eds. *The Recent Performance of the Italian Economy: Market Outcomes and State Policy.* Economia. Sezione 5. Ricerche di economia applicata, no. 30. Milan: Angeli, 1991.

1165. Castronovo, Valerio. *Storia di una banca: La Banca nazionale del lavoro e lo sviluppo economico italiano, 1913–1983.* Biblioteca di cultura storica, no. 151. Torino: G. Einaudi, 1983.

1166. Gambetta, Diego. *The Sicilian Mafia: The Business of Private Protection*. Cambridge: Harvard University Press, 1993.

1167. Giavazzi, Francesco, and Luigi Spaventa, eds. *High Public Debt: The Italian Experience*. Cambridge and New York: Cambridge University Press, 1988.

1168. Mayer, Thomas, and Franco Spinelli, eds. *Macroeconomics and Macroeconomic Policy Issues*. Aldershot, Hampshire, and Brookfield, Vt.: Avebury; and Brookfield, Vt.: Gower, 1991.

1169. Podbielski, Gisele. *Italy, Development and Crisis in the Post-War Economy*. Economies of the World. Oxford: Clarendon Press, 1974.

1170. Southard, Frank Allen. *The Finances of European Liberation with Special Reference to Italy*. International Finance. New York: Published for the Carnegie Endowment for International Peace by King's Crown Press, 1946. Reprint. New York: Arno Press, 1978.

1171. Zamagni, Vera. *The Economic History of Italy, 1860–1990*. New York: Clarendon Press; and Oxford: Oxford University Press, 1993. Originally published as *Dalla periferia al centro*.

Italy—Emigration and Immigration

1172. Blackstone, Roger. *The Salt of Another's Bread: Immigration Control and the Social Impact of Immigration in Italy: Report of a Western European Union Study Visit*. London: Home Office, 1989.

1173. Briani, Vittorio. *Italian Immigrants Abroad: A Bibliography on the Italian Experience Outside Italy in Europe, the Americas, Australia, and Africa*. Detroit: B. Ethridge Books, 1979.

1174. Iraci Fedeli, Leone. *Razzismo e immigrazione, il caso Italia*. Primopiano, no. 1. Roma: Edizioni Acropoli, 1990.

Italy—European Community Relations

1175. Carello, Adrian Nicola. *The Northern Question: Italy's Participation in the European Economic Community and the Mezzogiorno's Underdevelopment*. Newark: University of Delaware Press; and London and Cranbury, N.J.: Associated University Presses, 1989.

1176. Francioni, Francesco, ed. *Italy and EC Membership Evaluated*. EC Membership Evaluated Series. New York: St. Martin's Press, 1992.

Italy—Foreign Relations

1177. Campbell, John Coert, ed. *Successful Negotiation, Trieste 1954: An Appraisal by the Five Participants*. Princeton: Princeton University Press, 1976.

1178. Cassels, Alan. *Italian Foreign Policy, 1918–1945: A Guide to Research and Research Materials*. Rev. ed. Guides to European Diplomatic History Research and Research Materials. Wilmington: Scholarly Resources, 1991.

1179. De Franciscis, Maria Elisabetta. *Italy and the Vatican: The 1984 Concordat Between Church and State*. Studies in Modern European History, no. 2. New York: P. Lang, 1989.

1180. Harper, John Lamberton. *America and the Reconstruction of Italy, 1945–1948*. Cambridge and New York: Cambridge University Press, 1986.

1181. Hughes, Henry Stuart. *The United States and Italy*. 3d ed. American Foreign Policy Library. Cambridge: Harvard University Press, 1979.

1182. Smith, E. Timothy. *The United States, Italy, and NATO, 1947–52*. New York: St. Martin's Press, 1991.

1183. Wollemborg, Leo J. *Stars, Stripes, and Italian Tricolor: The United States and Italy, 1946–1989*. New York: Praeger, 1990.

Italy—History

1184. Baranski, Zygmunt G., and Robert Lumley, eds. *Culture and Conflict in Postwar Italy: Essays on Mass and Popular Culture*. University of Reading European and International Studies. Houdmills, Basingstoke: Macmillan, in association with the Graduate School of European and International Studies, University of Reading, 1990.

1185. Barzini, Luigi. *The Italians*. New York: Atheneum, 1977.

1186. Bowman, Alfred Connor. *Zones of Strain: A Memoir of the Early Cold War*. Hoover Press Publication, no. 273. Stanford: Hoover Institution Press, 1982.

1187. Brooker, Paul. *The Faces of Fraternalism: Nazi Germany, Fascist Italy, and Imperial Japan*. Oxford: Clarendon Press; and New York: Oxford University Press, 1991.

1188. Castronovo, Valerio, ed. *L'Italia contemporanea, 1945–1975*. Torino: G. Einaudi, 1976.

1189. Churchill, Winston. *Closing the Ring*. Chartwell ed. The Second World War, v. 5. Boston: Houghton Mifflin, 1983.

1190. Ginsborg, Paul. *A History of Contemporary Italy: Society and Politics, 1943–1988*. Penguin History. London and New York: Penguin Books, 1990.

1191. Lange, Peter Michael, George Ross, and Maurizio Vannicelli. *Unions, Change, and Crisis: French and Italian Union Strategy and the Political Economy, 1945–80*. London and New York: Allen and Unwin, 1982.

1192. Passerini, Luisa. *Facism in Popular Memory: The Cultural Experience of the Turin Working Class*. Translated by Robert Lumley and Jude Bloomfield. Cambridge and New York: Cambridge University Press, 1987. Originally published as *Torino operaia e fascismo*.

1193. White, Steven F. *Progressive Renaissance: America and the Reconstruction of Italian Education, 1943–1962*. Modern European History. Italy. New York: Garland, 1991.

1194. Wiskemann, Elizabeth. *Italy Since 1945*. London: Macmillan; and New York: St. Martin's Press, 1971.

1195. Woolf, Stuart Joseph, ed. *The Rebirth of Italy, 1943–1950*. London: Longmans, 1972.

Italy—Language

1196. Lepschy, Anna Laura, and Giulio Lepschy. *The Italian Language Today*. 2d ed. London and New York: Routledge, 1992.

1197. Maiden, Martin. *A Linguistic History of Italian*. London and New York: Longman, 1994.

Italy—Literature

1198. Arico, Santo L., ed. *Contemporary Women Writers in Italy: A Modern Renaissance*. Amherst: University of Massachusetts Press, 1990.

1199. Caesar, Michael, and Peter Hainsworth, eds. *Writers & Society in Contemporary Italy: A Collection of Essays*. New York: St. Martin's Press, 1984.

1200. Pacifici, Sergio. *A Guide to Contemporary Italian Literature: From Futurism to Neorealism*. Carbondale: Southern Illinois University Press, 1972.

1201. Ragusa, Olga. *Narrative and Drama: Essays in Modern Italian Literature From Verga to Pasolini.* De Proprietatibus litterarum: Series practica, no. 110. The Hague: Mouton, 1976.

Italy—Music

1202. Brody, Elaine, and Claire Brook. *The Music Guide to Italy.* New York: Dodd, Mead, 1978.

1203. Respighi, Elsa. *Fifty Years of a Life in Music, 1905–1955.* Translated by Giovanni Fontecchio and Roger Johnson. Studies in the History and Interpretation of Music, no. 42. Lewiston, N.Y.: E. Mellen Press, 1993. Originally published as *Cinquant anni di vita nella musica.*

Italy—Politics and Government

1204. Baker, John Alexander. *Italian Communism: The Road to Legitimacy and Autonomy.* Washington, D.C.: National Defense University Press, 1989.

1205. Di Palma, Giuseppe. *Surviving Without Governing: The Italian Parties in Parliament.* Berkeley: University of California Press, 1977.

1206. Domenico, Roy Palmer. *Italian Fascists on Trial, 1943–1948.* Chapel Hill: University of North Carolina Press, 1991.

1207. Hine, David. *Governing Italy: The Politics of Bargained Pluralism.* Oxford: Clarendon Press; and New York: Oxford University Press, 1993.

1208. Kogan, Norman. *A Political History of Italy: The Postwar Years.* New York: Praeger, 1983.

1209. Leonardi, Robert, and Douglas A. Wertman. *Italian Christian Democracy: The Politics of Dominance.* Houndmills, Basingstoke: Macmillan, 1989,

1210. Pantaleone, Michele. *Mafia e politica.* 5 ed. Torino: Einaudi, 1978.

1211. Pridham, Geoffrey. *Political Parties and Coalitional Behaviour in Italy.* London and New York: Routledge, 1988.

1212. Putnam, Robert D. *Making Democracy Work: Civic Traditions in Modern Italy.* Princeton: Princeton University Press, 1993.

1213. Tarrow, Sidney G. *Democracy and Disorder: Protest and Politics in Italy, 1965–1975.* Oxford: Clarendon Press; and New York: Oxford University Press, 1989.

Italy—Religion

1214. Giammanco, Rosanna Mulazzi. *The Catholic-Communist Dialogue in Italy: 1944 to the Present.* New York: Praeger, 1989.

1215. Kent, Peter C. *The Pope and the Duce: The International Impact of the Lateran Agreements.* New York: St. Martin's Press, 1981.

1216. Kertzer, David I. *Comrades and Christians: Religion and Political Struggle in Communist Italy.* Cambridge and New York: Cambridge University Press, 1980.

1217. Levi, Primo. *The Reawakening.* Translated by Stuart Woolf. New York: Macmillan, 1993. Originally published as *Tregua.*

1218. Sacerdoti, Annie, and Luca Fiorentino. *Guide to Jewish Italy.* Translated by Richard F. De Lossa. Brooklyn: Israelowitz, 1989. Originally published as: *Guida all'Italia ebraica.*

1219. Wolff, Richard J. *Between Pope and Duce: Catholic Students in Fascist Italy.* Studies in Modern European History, no. 1. New York: P. Lang, 1990.

LIECHTENSTEIN

Liechtenstein—Economics

1220. Biedermann, Klaus. *The Trust in Liechtenstein Law.* Translated by H. Gerald Crossland. Oxford: Alvescot Press, 1984. Originally published as *Die Treuhänderschaft des liechtensteinischen Rechts.*

1221. Marxer, Peter. *Companies and Taxes in Liechtenstein.* Liechtenstein and San Francisco: Austin & Winfield, 1992.

Liechtenstein—European Community Relations

1222. European Economic Community. *Agreement Between the European Economic Community and the Swiss Confederation: With Final Act, Additional Agreement Concerning the Validity of the Agreement for Liechtenstein.* London: H.M.S.O., 1972.

Liechtenstein—History

1223. Kranz, Walter, ed. *The Principality of Liechtenstein.* 5th ed. Vaduz: Press and Information Office, Principality of Liechtenstein, 1981. Originally published as: *Fürstentum Liechtenstein.*

1224. Raton, Pierre. *Liechtenstein; History and Institutions of the Principality.* Vaduz: Liechtenstein-Verlag, 1970. Originally published as *Le Liechtenstein, histoire et institutions.* 2d ed. 1967.

1225. Schlapp, Manfred. *This is Liechtenstein.* Stuttgart: Seewald, 1980. Originally published as *Das ist Liechtenstein.*

LUXEMBOURG

Luxembourg—Cultural Life

1226. Bibliothèque nationale de Luxembourg. *La Bibliothèque nationale de Luxembourg.* Luxembourg: La Bibliothèque, 1987.

1227. Brody, Elaine, and Claire Brook. *The Music Guide to Belgium, Luxembourg, Holland, and Switzerland.* New York: Dodd, Mead, 1977.

1228. Jank, Pia. *Gravures luxembourgeoises: Catalogue des gravures, lithographies et serigraphies luxembourgeoises conservées à la Bibliothèque nationale de Luxembourg.* Luxembourg: La Bibliothèque, 1991.

1229. Moll, Udo. *Luxemburg.* DuMont-Kunst-Reiseführer. Köln: DuMont, 1983.

1230. Sagrillo, Damien. *Untersuchungen zum luxemburgischen Volkslied.* Köln: Universität zu Köln, 1987.

Luxembourg—Economics

1231. Als, Georges. *Histoire quantitative du Luxembourg: 1839–1990.* Cahiers économiques, no. 79. Luxembourg: Service central de la statistique et des études économiques, 1991.

1232. Dargent, Jean. *Luxembourg, an International Financial Centre.* Translated by Fernand Rau. Acquaintance with Luxembourg, no. 5. Luxembourg: Ministry of State Information and Press Dept., 1972.

1233. Desmit, Bart. *Les conséquences économiques de l'abolition de l'association monétaire belgo-luxembourgeoise.* Genève: Institut universitaire de hautes études internationales, 1989.

1234. Ries, Adrien. *L'Agriculture luxembourgeoise dans le marché commun.* Cahiers économiques, no. 45. Luxembourg: Service central de la statistique et des études économiques, 1970.

1235. Siebertz, Jean, and Monique Haidon. *Le Sud-Luxembourg.* Courrier hebdomadaire du CRISP, nos. 695–696. 2 vols. Bruxelles: CRISP, 1975.

Luxembourg—European Community Relations

1236. Luxembourg. Ministry of State. Press and Information Service. *La Présidence luxembourgeoise des Communautés européennes: 1er janvier 1991 au 30 juin 1991.* 2 vols. Luxembourg: Le Service, 1991.

Luxembourg—Foreign Relations

1237. Dollar, Jacques. *Les Luxembourgeois et la France: De Poincaré à Pompidou*. 3 éd. Luxembourg: Impr. Saint-Paul, 1976.

1238. Poidevin, Raymond, and Gilbert Trausch. *Les Relations franco-luxembourgeoises de Louis XIV à Robert Schuman*. Publications du Centre de recherches Relations internationales de l'Université de Metz, no. 11. Metz: Université de Metz, Centre de recherches Relations internationales, Faculté des lettres, 1978.

Luxembourg—Geography

1239. Schmit, Guy, and Bernd Wiese. *Luxemburg in Karte und Luft-bild=Le Luxembourg en cartes et photos aériennes*. Luxembourg: Editions Guy Schmit & Bernd Wiese, 1980.

Luxembourg—History

1240. Als, Georges. *Luxembourg: Historic, Geographic, and Economic Profile*. Luxembourg: Service Information et Presse, 1978. Originally published as *Luxembourg: Profil historique, géographique, économique*.

1241. Hury, Carlo, and Jules Christophory. *Luxembourg*. World Bibliographical Series, no. 23. Oxford and Santa Barbara: Clio Press, 1981.

1242. Newcomer, James. *The Grand Duchy of Luxembourg: The Evolution of Nationhood, 963 A.D. to 1983*. Lanham, Md.: University Press of America; and Fort Worth: Texas Christian University, 1984.

1243. Petit, Joseph. *Luxembourg, Yesterday and To-Day*. Luxembourg: Printed by P. Linden, Printer of the Grand Ducal Court, 196-?.

1244. Remy. *Histoires de la résistance en Lorraine & au Grand-Duché de Luxembourg*. 2 vols. Genève: Famot, 1974.

1245. Rossomme-Lauwens, Gilberte, Margarete Stillger, and Jean Modot. *Belgique, Luxembourg*. Les Guides bleus. Paris: Hachette, 1979.

1246. Tomes, John, ed. *Belgium and Luxembourg*. 5th ed. The Blue Guides. London: E. Benn; and Chicago: Rand McNally, 1977.

Luxembourg—Immigration

1247. Spineux, Armand. *Vocational Training of Young Migrants in Luxembourg*. CEDEFOP Document. Berlin: European Centre for the Development of Vocational Training, 1986.

Luxembourg—Language

1248. Davis, Kathryn Anne. *Language Planning in Multilingual Contexts: Policies, Communities, and Schools in Luxembourg*. Studies in Bilingualism, no. 8. Amsterdam and Philadelphia: J. Benjamins, 1994.

1249. Goudaillier, Jean-Pierre. *Phonologie fonctionnelle et phonétique expérimentale: Exemples empruntés au luxemburgeois*. Hamburger phonetische Beiträge, Bd. 36. Hamburg: H. Buske, 1981.

1250. Hoffmann, Fernand. *Sprachen in Luxemburg*. Beiträge zur luxemburgischen Sprach- und Volkskunde, nr. 12. Luxembourg: Institut Grand-Ducal, Section de linguistique, de folklore et de typonomie, 1979.

Luxembourg—Politics and Government

1251. Luxembourg. Ministry of State. Press, and Information Service. *The Luxembourg Grand Ducal Family*. Luxembourg: The Ministry, 1990.

1252. Majerus, Pierre. *The Institutions of the Grand Duchy of Luxembourg*. Luxembourg: Ministry of State, Press, and Information Service, 1989.

MALTA

Malta—Architecture

1253. Knevitt, Charles. *Connections: The Architecture of Richard England, 1964–84*. London: Lund Humphries, 1984.

Malta—Bibliography

1254. Sciberras, Lillian, and Marlene Saliba. *The Maltese Woman: A Bibliography of Recent Literature*. Msida: University of Malta Library, 1975.

1255. Sapienza, Anthony F. *A Checklist of Maltese Periodicals and Newspapers in the National Library of Malta and the University of Malta Library*. Valletta: Malta University Press, 1977.

1256. Xuereb, Paul. *A Bibliography of Maltese Bibliographies*. Msida: University of Malta Library, 1978.

Malta—Economics

1257. Baldacchino, Godfrey. *Worker Cooperatives with Particular Reference to Malta*. Occasional Paper; no. 107. The Hague: Institute of Social Studies, 1990.

1258. Bonanno, Nicolas S. *Capital, Accumulation, and Economic Growth: In Theory and as They Relate in the Maltese Paradigm.* Documents économiques; no. 44. Fribourg: Editions Universitaires Fribourg, 1989.

1259. Cremona, F. *The Law on Commercial Partnerships in Malta.* Msida: University of Malta, 1989.

1260. Kester, Gerard. *Transition to Workers' Self-Management: Its Dynamics in the Decolonizing Economy of Malta.* Research Report Series—Institute of Social Studies; no. 7. The Hague: Institute of Social Studies, 1980.

1261. Spiteri, Patrick, and Henri Mizzi. *Malta: International Tax Planning.* Longman Intelligence Reports. London: Longman, 1989.

Malta—European Community Relations

1262. Redmond, John. *The Next Mediterranean Enlargement of the European Community: Turkey, Cyprus, and Malta?* Aldershot, Hampshire, and Brookfield, Vt.: Dartmouth, 1993.

Malta—History

1263. Caruana, Carmen M. *Education's Role in the Socioeconomic Development of Malta.* Westport: Praeger, 1992.

1264. Cuschieri, Carmel. *Index historicus: A Classified Index of Articles . . . Relating to Maltese History . . .* Malta: The Author, 1979.

1265. Mallia-Milanes, Victor, ed. *The British Colonial Experience, 1800–1964: The Impact on Maltese Society.* Msida: Mireva Publications, 1988.

1266. Thackrah, John Richard. *Malta.* World Bibliographical Series; no. 64. Oxford and Santa Barbara: Clio Press, 1985.

Malta—Language

1267. Marshall, David R. *History of the Maltese Language in Local Education.* Msida: Malta University Press, 1971.

Malta—Migration

1268. King, Russell. *The Maltese Migration Cycle: Perspectives on Return.* Discussion Paper in Geography; no. 13. Oxford: Oxford Polytechnic, 1980.

Malta—Politics and Government

1269. Frendo, Henry. *Party Politics in a Fortress Colony*. Maltese Social Studies; no. 5. Valletta: Midsea Books, 1979.

1270. York, Barry. *Malta: a Non-Aligned Democracy in the Mediterranean*. Sydney: University of Sydney, 1987.

Malta—Religion

1271. Debrincat, Saviour. *Church and Family in Malta*. Rome: Pontificia Universitas Lateranensis, Facultas Theologiae, 1985.

1272. Koster, Adrianus. *Prelates and Politicians in Malta: Changing Power-Balances Between Church and State in a Mediterranean Island Fortress, 1800–1976*. Studies in Developing Countries; no. 29. Assen: Van Gorcum, 1984.

1273. Mintoff, Dom, ed. *Malta: Church, State, Labour*. Malta: Malta Labour Party, 1966.

1274. Vassallo, Mario. *From Lordship to Stewardship: Religion and Social Change in Malta*. Religion and Society; no. 15. The Hague: Mouton, 1979.

MONACO

Monaco—Bibliography

1275. Lavagna, Paul. *Bibliographie nationale de la principauté de Monaco, 1761–1986*. Monaco: Testa, 1988.

Monaco—Business and Economics

1276. Douvier, Pierre-Jean. *Monaco Tax and Legal Guide*. Deventer; Boston: Kluwer Law and Taxation Publishers; Paris: F. Lefebvre, 1991.

1277. Fielding, Xan. *The Money Spinner: Monte Carlo Casino*. London: Weidenfeld and Nicolson, 1977.

Monaco—Government

1278. Grinda, Georges. *Les institutions de la principauté de Monaco*. 2e éd. Monaco: Conseil national, 1975.

Monaco—History

1279. Edwards, Anne. *The Grimaldis of Monaco*. New York: Morrow, 1992.

1280. Hudson, Grace L. *Monaco*. World Bibliographical Series, no. 120. Oxford and Santa Barbara: Clio Press, 1991.

1281. Jackson, Stanley. *Inside Monte Carlo*. London: W. H. Allen, 1975.

1282. Robert, Jean Baptiste. *Histoire de Monaco*. Que sais-je? no. 1497. Paris: Presses universitaires de France, 1973.

1283. Robinson, Jeffrey. *Rainier & Grace*. London and New York: Simon & Schuster, 1989.

Monaco—Numismatics

1284. Vos, Raymond de. *History of the Monies, Medals, and Tokens of Monaco, 1640–1977*. Monaco: Testa, 1977.

NETHERLANDS

Netherlands—Art

1285. Babel Translations. *Holland: A Phaidon Art and Architecture Guide*. Translated and edited by Babel Translations. New York: Prentice-Hall Press, 1987. Originally published as Knaurs Kulturführer in Farbe.

1286. Neff, John Hallmark. *Contemporary Art From the Netherlands: An Exhibition*. Amsterdam: Visual Arts Office for Abroad of the Netherlands Ministry for Cultural Affairs, Recreation, and Social Welfare, 1982.

1287. Nieuwendijk, Koen. *The Refined Image: Aspects of Dutch New Realist Painting*. Amsterdam: Gallery Lieve Hemel, 1985.

1288. Raaij, Stefan van, ed. *Imitation and Inspiration: Japanese Influence on Dutch Art*. Amsterdam: Art Unlimited Books, 1989.

1289. Wilson, John Montgomery. *Dutch Art & Modern Life, 1882–1982*. Holland, Mich.: De Pree Art Center & Gallery, 1982.

Netherlands—Colonialism

1290. Coolhaas, W. Philippus. *A Critical Survey of Studies on Dutch Colonial History*. 2d ed. Bibliographical Series (Koninklijk Instituut voor Taal-, Land- en Volkenkunde); no. 4. The Hague: M. Nijhoff, 1980.

1291. McKay, Vernon. *Empires in Transition: British, French and Dutch Colonial Plans*. New York: Foreign Policy Association, 1947.

1292. Royal Institute of International Affairs. Information Dept. *Nether-lands Overseas Territories.* London: The Royal Institute of International Affairs. New York: Oxford University Press, 1941.

1293. Taylor, Jean Gelman. *The Social World of Batavia: European and Eurasian in Dutch Asia.* Madison: University of Wisconsin Press, 1983.

1294. United States. Library of Congress, Netherlands Studies Unit. *A Guide to Dutch Bibliographies.* Washington, D.C.: The Library, 1951.

1295. Wesseling, H. L. *Indie verloren, rampspoed geboren.* Amsterdam: B. Bakker, 1988.

Netherlands—Economics

1296. Dutt, Ashok K., and Frank J. Costa, eds. *Public Planning in the Netherlands: Perspectives and Change Since the Second World War.* New York: Oxford University Press, 1985.

1297. Griffiths, Richard T., ed. *The Economy and Politics of the Netherlands Since 1945.* The Hague: M. Nijhoff, 1980.

1298. Kuik, Onno, and Harmen Verbruggen, eds. *In Search of Indicators of Sustainable Development.* Environment & Management, no. 1. Dordrecht and Boston: Kluwer Academic Publishers, 1991.

Netherlands—European Community Relations

1299. Bos, Jan Marinus Meeuwis. *Dutch EC Policy Making: A Model-Guided Approach to Coordination and Negotiation.* Amsterdam: Thesis Publishers, 1991.

1300. Wolters, Menno, and Peter Coffey, eds. *The Netherlands and EC Membership Evaluated.* EC Membership Evaluated Series. New York: St. Martin's Press, 1990.

Netherlands—Foreign Relations

1301. Everts, Philip P. *Public Opinion, the Churches, and Foreign Policy.* Leiden: Institute for International Studies, University of Leiden, 1983.

1302. Everts, Philip P., ed. *Controversies at Home: Domestic Factors in the Foreign Policy of the Netherlands.* Dordrecht and Boston: M. Nijhoff, 1985.

1303. Heldring, Jerome. *Changes in Dutch Society and their Implications for Netherlands-South African Relations.* Occasional Paper (South African Institute of International Affairs). Braamfontein, South Africa: The Institute, 1984.

1304. Kuyper, Pieter Jan. *The Implementation of International Sanctions: The Netherlands and Rhodesia.* Alphen aan den Rijn: Sijthoff & Noordhoff, 1978.

1305. Leurdijk, J. H., ed. *The Foreign Policy of the Netherlands.* Alphen aan den Rijn: Sijthoff & Noordhoff, 1978.

Netherlands—Immigration

1306. Amersfoort, Hans van. *Immigration and the Formation of Minority Groups: The Dutch Experience, 1945–1975.* Translated by Robert Lyng. Cambridge and New York: Cambridge University Press, 1982. Originally published as *Immigratie en minderheidsvorming.*

1307. Brock, Colin, ed. *The Caribbean in Europe: Aspects of the West Indian Experience in Britain, France, and the Netherlands.* London and Totowa, N.J.: F. Cass, 1986.

1308. Cross, Malcom, and Han Entzinger, eds. *Lost Illusions: Caribbean Minorities in Britain and the Netherlands.* London: Routledge, 1988.

Netherlands—Language

1309. Entjes, H. *Dialecten in Nederland.* Haren-Gn.: Knoop & Niemeijer, 1974.

1310. Extra, Guus, and Ton Vallen. *Ethnic Minorities and Dutch as a Second language.* Studies on language acquisition, no. 1. Dordrecht and Cinnaminson, U.S.A.: Fortis Publications, 1985.

Netherlands—Literature

1311. Meijer, Reinder P. *Dutch and Flemish—Two Literatures or One?* London: Bedford College, University of London, 1973.

1312. Snapper, Johan P. *Post-War Dutch Literature: A Harp Full of Nails.* Amsterdam: Delta, 1971.

1313. Snapper, Johan P., and Thomas F. Shannon, eds. *The Berkeley Conference on Dutch Literature 1991: Europe 1992, Dutch Literature in an International Context.* Publications of the American

Association for Netherlandic Studies, no. 6. Lanham: University Press of America, 1993.

1314. Snapper, Johan P., and Thomas F. Shannon, eds. *The Berkeley Conference on Dutch Literature 1987: New Perspectives on the Modern Period.* Publications of the American Association for Netherlandic Studies, no. 2. Lanham: University Press of America, 1989.

1315. Vermij, Lucie Th., and Martje Breedt Bruyn, eds. *Women Writers From the Netherlands and Flanders.* Translated by Greta Kilburn. Amsterdam: International Feminist Book Fair Press, 1992.

Netherlands—Music

1316. Samama, Leo, Fer Abrahams, and Michiel De Ruyter. *Music in the Netherlands.* Netherlands: Dutch Arts. Dept. of International Relations, Ministry of Cultural Affairs, 1985.

1317. Stichting Donemus. *General Catalogue.* 3 Vols. Amsterdam: Donemus Amsterdam, 1982.

Netherlands—Politics and Government

1318. Andeweg, R. B., and Galen A. Irwin. *Dutch Government and Politics.* New York: St. Martin's Press, 1993.

1319. Lijphart, Arend. *The Politics of Accommodation: Pluralism and Democracy in the Netherlands.* 2d ed. Berkeley: University of California Press, 1975.

1320. Tash, Robert C. *Dutch Pluralism: A Model in Tolerance for Developing Countries.* Intercultural Studies, no. 1. New York: P. Lang, 1991.

Netherlands—Religion

1321. Benjamin, Yigael. *They Were Our Friends: A Memorial for the Members of the Hachsharot and the Hehalutz Underground in Holland Murdered in the Holocaust.* Jerusalem: Association of Former Members of the Hachsharot and the Hehalutz Underground in Holland, Westerweel Group included, 1990.

1322. Coleman, John Aloysius. *The Evolution of Dutch Catholicism, 1958–1974.* Berkeley: University of California, 1978.

1323. Goddijn, Walter. *The Deferred Revolution: A Social Experiment in Church Innovation in Holland, 1960–1970.* Amsterdam and New York: Elsevier Scientific Pub. Co., 1975.

1324. Stein, Andre. *Quiet Heroes: True Stories of the Rescue of Jews by Christians in Nazi-Occupied Holland.* New York: New York University Press, 1988.

NORWAY

Norway—Architecture

1325. Norberg-Schulz, Christian. *Modern Norwegian Architecture.* Oslo: Norwegian University Press, 1986.

1326. Thiis-Evensen, Thomas. *The Postmodernists Jan & Jon.* Translated by Sandra Hamilton. Norwegian Architects. Oslo: Universitetsforlaget, 1984.

Norway—Economics

1327. Hodne, Fritz. *The Norwegian Economy, 1920–1980.* London: Croom Helm; New York: St. Martin's Press, 1983.

1328. Knudsen, Ole. *Norway at Work: A Survey of the Principal Branches of the Economy.* Tanum's Tokens of Norway. Oslo: J. G. Tanum Forlag, 1972.

Norway—European Community Relations

1329. Allen, Hilary. *Norway and Europe in the 1970s.* Norwegian Foreign Policy Studies, no. 27. Oslo: Universitetsforlaget, 1979.

1330. European Movement in Norway. *Norway's Security and European Foreign Policy in the 1980s.* Oslo: Universitetsforlaget, 1981.

1331. Nelsen, Brent F., ed. *Norway and the European Community: The Political Economy of Integration.* Westport, Conn.: Praeger, 1993.

1332. Orvik, Nils, Daniel Heradstveit, and David L. Larson. *Norway's No to Europe.* Occasional Paper, no. 5. Pittsburgh: International Studies Association, 1975.

Norway—Foreign Relations

1333. Ausland, John C. *Norway, Oil, and Foreign Policy.* A Westview Special Study. Boulder: Westview Press, 1979.

1334. Cole, Wayne S. *Norway and the United States, 1905–1955: Two Democracies in Peace and War.* Ames: Iowa State University Press, 1989.

1335. Egeland, Jan. *Impotent Superpower—Potent Small State: Potentials and Limitations of Human Rights Objectives in the Foreign Policies of the United States and Norway.* Oslo: Universitetsforlaget, 1988.

1336. Floistad, Brit. *Fish and Foreign Policy: Norway's Fisheries Policy Towards Other Countries in the Barents Sea, the Norwegian Sea, and the North Sea.* Occasional Paper, no. 37. Honolulu: Law of the Sea Institute, W. S. Richardson School of Law, University of Hawaii, 1991. Originally published as *Fisk og utenrikspolitikk.*

1337. Holst, Johan Jorgen, ed. *Norwegian Foreign Policy in the 1980s.* Norwegian Foreign Policy Studies, no. 51. Oslo: Universitetsforlaget, 1985.

1338. Hveem, Helge. *International Relations and World Images: A Study of Norwegian Foreign Policy Elites.* PRIO Monographs from the International Peace Research Institute; no. 3. Oslo: Universitetsforlaget, 1972.

1339. Tamnes, Rolf. *The United States and the Cold War in the High North.* Aldershot, Hampshire, and Brookfield, Vt.: Dartmouth, 1991.

Norway—History

1340. Hoidal, Oddvar K. *Quisling: A Study in Treason.* Oslo: Universitetsforlaget, 1989.

1341. Riste, Olav, and Berit Nokleby. *Norway 1940–45: The Resistance Movement.* Tanum's Tokens of Norway. Oslo: Tanum, 1970.

1342. Romsoy, Natalie Rogoff, ed. *Norwegian Society.* Translated by Susan Hoivik. Oslo: Universitetsforlaget; and New York: Humanities Press, 1974. Originally published as: *Det norske samfunn.*

1343. Selbyg, Arne. *Norway Today: An Introduction to Modern Norwegian Society.* Oslo: Universitetsforlaget, 1986.

Norway—Literature

1344. Garton, Janet. *Norwegian Women's Writing, 1850–1990.* Women in Context. London and Atlantic Highlands, N.J.: Athlone, 1993.

1345. Nass, Harald S., ed. *A History of Norwegian Literature.* A History of Scandinavian Literature, no. 2. Lincoln: University of Nebraska Press in cooperation with the American-Scandinavian Foundation, 1993.

1346. Nass, Harald S. *Norwegian Literary Bibliography, 1956–1970.* Norsk bibliografisk bibliotek, Bd. 50. Oslo: Universitetsforlaget, 1975.

1347. Romskaug, Brenda, and Reidar Romskaug, eds. *Norwegian Fairy Tales.* London: University of London Press, 1964.

Norway—Politics and Government

1348. Arntzen, Jon Gunnar, and Bard Bredrup Knudsen. *Political Life and Institutions in Norway.* Oslo: International Summer School, University of Oslo, 1981.

1349. Eckstein, Harry. *Division and Cohesion in Democracy: A Study of Norway.* Princeton: Princeton University Press, 1966.

1350. Listhaug, Ola. *Citizens, Parties, and Norwegian Electoral Politics, 1957–1985.* Trondheim: Tapir, 1989.

1351. Olsen, Johan P. *Organized Democracy: Political Institutions in a Welfare State, the Case of Norway.* Bergen and Oslo: Universitetsforlaget, 1983.

1352. Omrcanin, Margaret Stewart. *Norway, Sweden, Croatia: A Comparative Study of State Secession and Formation.* Philadelphia: Dorrance, 1976.

Norway—Religion

1353. Hale, Frederick. *Norwegian Religious Pluralism: A Trans-Atlantic Comparison.* Text and Studies in Religion, no. 59. Lewiston, N.Y.: E. Mellen Press, 1992.

Norway—Social Structures

1354. Higley, John, George Lowell Field, and Knut Groholt. *Elite Structure and Ideology: A Theory with Applications to Norway.* Oslo: Universitetsforlaget; and New York: Columbia University Press, 1976.

1355. Holter, Harriet, ed. *Patriarchy in a Welfare Society.* Oslo: Universitetsforlaget, 1984.

1356. Jonassen, Christen Tonnes. *Value Systems and Personality in a Western Civilization: Norwegians in Europe and America.* Columbus: Ohio State University Press, 1983.

1357. Martinussen, Willy. *The Distant Democracy: Social Inequality, Political Resources and Political Influence in Norway.* London; New York: Wiley, 1977. Originally published as *Fjerndemokratiet.*

PORTUGAL

Portugal—Art

1358. Tannock, Michael. *Portuguese 20th Century Artists: A Biographical Dictionary.* Chichester, U.K.: Phillimore, 1978.

Portugal—Colonialism

1359. Bender, Gerald J. *Angola Under the Portuguese: The Myth and the Reality.* Perspectives on Southern Africa, no. 23. Berkeley: University of California Press, 1978.

1360. Birmingham, David. *Frontline Nationalism in Angola and Mozambique.* London: James Currey, 1992.

1361. Chilcote, Ronald H., ed. *Emerging Nationalism in Portuguese Africa: Documents.* Hoover Institution Publications, no. 97. Stanford: Hoover Institution Press, 1972.

1362. Clarence-Smith, Gervase. *The Third Portuguese Empire, 1825–1975: A Study in Economic Imperialism.* Manchester, U.K., and Dover, N.H.: Manchester University Press, 1985.

1363. Lima, Maria Fernanda. *Obligations of Portugal as the Administering [sic] Power of the Non-Self Governing Territory of East Timor.* Lisboa: Assembleia da Republica, 1992. Originally published as: *Obrigações de Portugal como potencia administrante do territorio nao autonomo de Timor-Leste.*

1364. Newitt, Malyn. *Portugal in Africa: The Last Hundred Years.* London: C. Hurst, 1981.

1365. Pitcher, M. Anne. *Politics in the Portuguese Empire: The State, Industry, and Cotton, 1926–1974.* Oxford: Clarendon Press; and New York: Oxford University Press, 1993.

1366. United States. Congress. House. Committee on Foreign Affairs. Subcommittee on Africa. *The Complex of United States-Portuguese Relations: Before and After the Coup: Hearings Before the Subcommittee on Africa of the Committee on Foreign Affairs* ... Washington, D.C.: G.P.O., 1974.

Portugal—Economics

1367. Amaral, Joao Ferreira do, Diogo de Lucena, and Antonio Sampaio Mello, eds. *The Portuguese Economy Towards 1992.* Boston: Kluwer Academic Publishers, 1992.

1368. *Employment and Basic Needs in Portugal.* Geneva: International Labour Office, 1979.

1369. Gaspar, Jorge, and Allan Williams. *North and Central Portugal in the 1990s: A European Investment Region.* EIU European Investment Regions Series. London: Economist Intelligence Unit, 1991.

1370. Yannopoulos, George, ed. *European Integration and the Iberian Economies.* New York: St. Martin's Press, 1989.

Portugal—European Community Relations

1371. Lopes, Jose da Silva, ed. *Portugal and EC Membership Evaluated.* EC Membership Evaluated Series. London: Pinter Publishers; and New York: St. Martin's Press, 1994.

1372. Lopes, Jose da Silva, and Luis Miguel Beleza, eds. *Portugal and the Internal Market of the EEC.* Lisbon: Banco de Portugal, 1991.

Portugal—Foreign Relations

1373. MacDonald, Scott B. *European Destiny, Atlantic Transformations: Portuguese Foreign Policy Under the Second Republic, 1974–1992.* New Brunswick, N.J.: Transaction Publishers, 1992.

1374. Maxwell, Kenneth, ed. *Portuguese Defense and Foreign Policy Since Democratization.* Camoes Center Special Report, no. 3. New York: Camoes Center, 1991.

1375. Maxwell, Kenneth, and Michael H. Haltzel. *Portugal: Ancient Country, Young Democracy.* Washington, D.C.: Wilson Center Press, 1990.

Portugal—Geography

1376. Ribeiro, Orlando, Hermann Lautensach, and Suzanne Daveua. *Geografia de Portugal.* 4 vols. Lisboa: Edicoes J. Sa da Costa, 1987–1991.

Portugal—History

1377. Birmingham, David. *A Concise History of Portugal.* Cambridge: Cambridge University Press, 1993.

1378. Graham, Lawrence S., and Douglas L. Wheeler. *In Search of Modern Portugal: The Revolution and its Consequences.* Madison: University of Wisconsin Press, 1983.

1379. Kay, Hugh. *Salazar and Modern Portugal.* London: Eyre and Spottiswoode, 1970.

1380. Machado, Diamantino P. *The Structure of Portuguese Society: The Failure of Fascism.* New York: Praeger, 1991.

1381. Maxwell, Kenneth. *The Press and the Rebirth of Iberian Democracy.* Westport, Conn.: Greenwood Press, 1983.

1382. Maxwell, Kenneth, ed. *Portugal in the 1980s: Dilemmas of Democratic Consolidation.* Contributions in Political Science, no. 138. New York: Greenwood Press, 1986.

1383. Maxwell, Kenneth, and Michael H. Haltzel, eds. *Portugal: Ancient Country, Young Democracy.* Washington, D.C.: Wilson Center Press, 1990.

1384. Maxwell, Kenneth, and Scott C. Monje. *Portugal: The Constitution and the Consolidation of Democracy, 1976–1989.* New York: Camoes Center, 1991.

1385. Raby, David L. *Fascism and Resistance in Portugal.* Manchester, U.K. and New York: Manchester University Press, 1988.

Portugal—Language

1386. Castagnaro, R. Anthony. *A Portuguese Primer.* American University Studies. Series VI, Foreign Language Instruction, no. 9. New York: P. Lang, 1989.

Portugal—Literature

1387. Nunes, Maria Luisa. *Becoming True to Ourselves: Cultural Decolonization and National Identity in the Literature of the Portuguese-Speaking World.* Contributions to the Study of World Literature; no. 22. New York: Greenwood Press, 1987.

1388. Schneider, Marshall J., and Irwin Stern, eds. *Modern Spanish and Portuguese Literatures.* A Library of Literary Criticism. New York: Continuum, 1988.

Portugal—Migration

1389. Brettell, Caroline. *Men Who Migrate, Women Who Wait.* Princeton: Princeton University Press, 1986.

1390. Bruneau, Thomas C., Victor M. P. Da Rosa, and Alexandre Macleod. *Portugal in Development.* Social Sciences; no. 9. Ottawa: University of Ottawa Press, 1984.

Portugal—Politics and Government

1391. Bermeo, Nancy Gina. *The Revolution Within the Revolution: Workers' Control in Rural Portugal.* Princeton: Princeton University Press, 1986.

1392. Ferreira, Hugo Gil, and Michael W. Marshall. *Portugal's Revolution*. Cambridge and New York: Cambridge University Press, 1986.

1393. Janitschek, Hans. *Mario Soares*. New York: St. Martin's Press, 1986.

1394. Wiarda, Howard J. *Politics in Iberia: The Political Systems of Spain and Portugal*. HarperCollins Series in Comparative Politics. New York: HarperCollins College Publishers, 1993.

Portugal—Religion

1395. *Igreja e sociedade no Portugal Contemporaneo*. Studium generale. Estudos contemporaneos. Porto: Secretaria de Estado da Cultura. Centro de Estudos Humanisticos, 1979.

1396. Ricard, Robert. *Etudes sur l'histoire morale et religieuse du Portugal*. Paris: Fundação Calouste Gulbenkian, Centro Cultural Portugues, 1970.

SAN MARINO

1397. Carrick, Noel. *San Marino*. New York: Chelsea House, 1988.

1398. Rossi, Giuseppe. *The Republic of San Marino*. San Marino: Governmental Tourist Body, 1976.

SCOTLAND

Scotland—Art

1399. Hartley, Keith. *Scottish Art Since 1900*. London: National Galleries of Scotland in association with Lund Humphries, 1989.

Scotland—Economics

1400. King, David Neden. *Financial and Economic Aspects of Regionalism and Separatism*. Great Britain. Commission on the Constitution. Research Papers, no. 10. London: H.M.S.O., 1973.

1401. Mair, Douglas, ed. *The Scottish Contribution to Modern Economic Thought*. Aberdeen: Aberdeen University Press, 1990.

1402. McCrone, Gavin. *Scotland's Future: The Economics of Nationalism*. Oxford: Blackwell, 1969.

1403. Morison, Hugh. *The Regeneration of Local Economies*. Oxford: Clarendon Press and New York: Oxford University Press, 1987.

Scotland—European Community Relations

1404. Archer, Clive, and John Main, eds. *Scotland's Voice in International Affairs: The Overseas Representation of Scottish Interest, With Special Reference to the European Economic Community.* London: C. Hurst and Montreal: McGill-Queen's University Press for the Royal Institute of International Affairs, 1980.

1405. Waters, N., and I. Watson. *Scottish Local Authorities, Economic Development and the E.E.C.: Based on a Report to the Anglo-German Foundation for the Study of Industrial Society.* Research Paper, no. 8. Glasgow: Planning Exchange, 1980.

Scotland—History

1406. Brotherstone, Terry, ed. *Covenant, Charter, and Party: Traditions of Revolt and Protest in Modern Scottish History.* Aberdeen: Aberdeen University Press, 1989.

1407. Gronneberg, Roy, ed. *Island Futures: Scottish Devolution and Shetland's Constitutional Alternatives.* Sandwick: Thuleprint, 1978.

1408. Harvie, Christopher. *Cultural Weapons: Scotland and Survival in a New Europe.* Edinburgh: Polygon, 1992.

1409. Scott, Paul Henderson. *Towards Independence, Essays on Scotland.* Determinations. Edinburgh: Polygon, 1991.

1410. Smout, T. Christopher. *A Century of the Scottish People, 1830–1950.* New Haven: Yale University Press, 1986.

Scotland—Immigration

1411. Devine, Thomas Martin, ed. *Irish Immigrants and Scottish Society in the Nineteenth and Twentieth Centuries.* Edinburgh: J. Donald, 1991.

1412. Jackson, Anthony. *Way of Life: Integration and Immigration.* North Sea Oil Panel Occasional Paper, no. 12. London: Social Science Research Council, 1980.

Scotland—Language

1413. Mackinnon, Kenneth, and Morag MacDonald. *Ethnic Communities: The Transmission of Language and Culture in Harris and Barra: A Report to the Social Science Research Council.* Hatfield: School of Social Sciences, Hatfield Polytechnic, 1980.

1414. O'Murchu, Mairtin. *East Perthshire Gaelic: Social History, Phonology, Texts, and Lexicon.* Perthshire Gaelic, no. 1. Dublin: Dublin Institute for Advanced Studies, 1989.

Scotland—Literature

1415. Aitken, William Russell. *Scottish Literature in English and Scots: A Guide to Information Sources.* Gale Information Guide Library. American Literature, English Literature, and World Literatures in English Information Guide Series, no. 37. Detroit: Gale Research Co., 1982.

1416. Bold, Alan Norman. *Modern Scottish Literature.* London and New York: Longman, 1983.

1417. Craig, Cairns, ed. *The History of Scottish Literature.* 4 vols. Aberdeen: Aberdeen University Press, 1987–1989.

1418. *Location Register of Twentieth-Century English Literary Manuscripts and Letters: A Union List of Papers of Modern English, Irish, Scottish, and Welsh Authors in the British Isles.* 2 vols. Boston: G. K. Hall, 1988.

1419. Matthews, Hellen, ed. *A Hairst O'Words: New Writing From North-East Scotland.* Aberdeen: Aberdeen University Press, 1991.

Scotland—Music

1420. Brody, Elaine, and Claire Brook. *The Music Guide to Great Britain: England, Scotland, Wales, Ireland.* New York: Dodd, Mead, 1975.

1421. Scottish Arts Council. *Recordings of Artists Working in Scotland.* Edinburgh: The Council, 1978.

Scotland—Politics and Government

1422. Fry, Michael. *Patronage and Principle: A Political History of Modern Scotland.* Aberdeen: Aberdeen University Press, 1987.

1423. Kellas, James G. *The Scottish Political System.* 4th ed. Cambridge and New York: Cambridge University Press, 1989.

1424. Midwinter, Arthur F., Michael Keating, and James Mitchell. *Politics and Public Policy in Scotland.* Houndmills, Basingstoke: Macmillan, 1991.

1425. Moore, Chris, and Simon Booth. *Managing Competition: Meso-Corporatism, Pluralism, and the Negotiated Order in Scotland.*

Oxford: Clarendon Press; and New York: Oxford University Press, 1989.

Scotland—Religion

1426. Bruce, Steve. *No Pope of Rome: Anti-Catholicism in Modern Scotland.* Edinburgh: Mainstream Publishers, 1985.

1427. Herron, Andrew. *Kirk by Divine Right: Church and State, Peaceful Coexistence.* Baird Lecture, 1985. Edinburgh: Saint Andrew Press, 1985.

SPAIN

Spain—Art

1428. Dyckes, William, ed. *Contemporary Spanish Art.* New York: Art Digest, 1975.

1429. Rowell, Margit. *New Images from Spain.* New York: Solomon R. Guggenheim Foundation, 1980.

Spain—Economics

1430. Allard, Gayle, and Jose Bolorinos. *Spain to 2000.* EIU Economic Prospects Series. London and New York: Economist Intelligence Unit, 1992.

1431. Botero, Rodrigo. *Reflections on the Modernization of Spain.* Occasional Papers (International Center for Economic Growth), no. 29. San Francisco: ICS Press, 1992.

1432. Harrison, Joseph. *The Spanish Economy in the Twentieth Century.* Croom Helm Series on the Contemporary Economic History of Europe. London: Croom Helm, 1985.

1433. Yannopoulos, George, ed. *European Integration and the Iberian Economies.* New York: St. Martin's Press, 1989.

Spain—European Community Relations

1434. Almarcha Barbado, Maria Amparo, ed. *Spain and EC Membership Evaluated.* EC Membership Evaluated Series. London: Pinter Publishers; and New York: St. Martin's Press, 1993.

1435. Hudson, Mark, and Stan Rudcenko. *Spain to 1992: Joining Europe's Mainstream.* EIU Economic Prospects Series. London and New York: Economist Intelligence Unit, 1988.

1436. Preston, Paul, and Denis Smyth. *Spain, the EEC, and NATO.* Chatham House Papers, no. 22. London and Boston: Routledge & K. Paul for the Royal Institute of International Affairs, 1984.

1437. Salmon, Keith G. *The Modern Spanish Economy: Transformation and Integration into Europe.* London and New York: Pinter, 1991.

Spain—Foreign Relations

1438. Feis, Herbert. *The Spanish Story: Franco and the Nations at War.* New York: Norton, 1966. Reprint. Westport, Conn.: Greenwood Press, 1987.

1439. Pollack, Benny, and Graham Hunter. *The Paradox of Spanish Foreign Policy: Spain's International Relations from Franco to Democracy.* New York: St. Martin's Press, 1987.

1440. Wiarda, Howard J., ed. *Iberian-Latin American Connection: Implications for U.S. Foreign Policy.* Westview Special Studies on Latin America and the Caribbean. Boulder: Westview Press; and Washington, D.C.: American Enterprise Institute, 1986.

Spain—History

1441. Beevor, Antony. *The Spanish Civil War.* London: Orbis, 1982.

1442. Ellwood, Sheelagh M. *Franco.* Profiles in Power. London and New York: Longman, 1994.

1443. Fishman, Robert M. *Working-Class Organization and the Return to Democracy in Spain.* Ithaca: Cornell University Press, 1990.

1444. Hansen, Edward C. *Rural Catalonia. Under the Franco Regime: The Fate of Regional Culture Since the Spanish Civil War.* Cambridge and New York: Cambridge University Press, 1977.

1445. Higginbotham, Virginia. *Spanish Film Under Franco.* Austin: University of Texas Press, 1988.

1446. Hooper, John. *The Spaniards: A Portrait of the New Spain.* Rev. ed. Harmondsworth, Middlesex, and New York: Penguin Books, 1987.

1447. Lannon, Frances, and Paul Preston, eds. *Elites and Power in Twentieth-Century Spain.* Oxford: Clarendon Press; and New York: Oxford University Press, 1990.

Spain—Literature

1448. Abellán, José Luis. *La cultura en España.* Madrid: Cuadernos para el diálogo, 1971.

1449. Brown, Joan Lipman, ed. *Women Writers of Contemporary Spain*. Newark: University of Delaware Press and London and Cranbury, N.J.: Associated University Presses, 1991.

1450. Ilie, Paul. *Literature and Inner Exile: Authoritarian Spain, 1939–1975*. Baltimore: Johns Hopkins University Press, 1980.

1451. Mermall, Thomas. *The Rhetoric of Humanism: Spanish Culture after Ortega y Gasset*. Studies in the Literary Analysis of Hispanic Texts. New York: Bilingual Press, 1976.

1452. Patt, Beatrice P., ed. *Spanish Literature Since the Civil War*. New York: Dodd, Mead, 1973.

1453. Smith, Paul Julian. *Representing the Other: "Race," Text, and Gender in Spanish and Spanish American Narrative*. Oxford: Clarendon Press; and New York: Oxford University Press, 1992.

1454. Ward, Philip, ed. *The Oxford Companion to Spanish Literature*. Oxford: Clarendon Press, 1978.

Spain—Music

1455. Marco, Tomás. *Spanish Music in the Twentieth Century*. Translated by Cola Franzen. Cambridge: Harvard University Press, 1993. Originally published as *Historia de la musica española*.

Spain—Nationalism

1456. Clark, Robert P. *Negotiating with ETA: Obstacles to Peace in the Basque Country, 1975–1988*. Reno: University of Nevada Press, 1990.

1457. Johnston, Hank. *Tales of Nationalism: Catalonia, 1939–1979*. New Brunswick: Rutgers University, 1991.

1458. Moxon-Browne, Edward. *Spain and the ETA: The Bid for Basque Autonomy*. London: Centre for Security and Conflict Studies, 1987.

Spain—Politics and Government

1459. Clark, Robert P., and Michael H. Haltzel, eds. *Spain in the 1980s: The Democratic Transition and a New International Role*. Cambridge, Mass.: Ballinger, 1987.

1460. Dobson, Andrew. *An Introduction to the Politics and Philosophy of José Ortega y Gasset*. Cambridge Iberian and Latin American Studies. Cambridge and New York: Cambridge University Press, 1989.

1461. Gunther, Richard, Giacomo Sani, and Goldie Shabad. *Spain After Franco: The Making of a Competitive Party System.* Berkeley: University of California Press, 1988.

1462. Gunther, Richard, ed. *Politics, Society, and Democracy: the Case of Spain.* Boulder: Westview Press, 1993.

1463. Marichal, Juan. *El nuevo pensamiento político español.* México: Finisterre, 1966.

1464. Martinez, Robert Esteban. *Business and Democracy in Spain.* Westport, Conn.: Praeger, 1993.

1465. Payne, Stanley G. *The Franco Regime, 1936–1975.* Madison: University of Wisconsin Press, 1987.

1466. Perez Diaz, Victor. *The Return of Civil Society. The Emergence of Democratic Spain.* Cambridge: Harvard University Press, 1993.

1467. Wiarda, Howard J. *Politics in Iberia: The Political Systems of Spain and Portugal.* HarperCollins Series in Comparative Politics. New York: HarperCollins College Publishers, 1993.

SWEDEN

Sweden—Art

1468. Ericson, Deborah. *In the Stockholm Art World.* Stockholm Studies in Social Anthropology, no. 17. Stockholm: University of Stockholm, Dept. of Social Anthropology, 1988.

1469. Notini, Anja. *Made in Sweden: Arts, Handicrafts, Design.* Westport, Conn.: Meckler Books, 1988.

Sweden—Decolonization

1470. Huldt, Bo. *Sweden, the United Nations and Decolonization: A Study of Swedish Participation in the Fourth Committee of the General Assembly, 1945–69.* Lund Studies in International History, no. 5. Stockholm: Esselte Studium, 1974.

Sweden—Economics

1471. Davidson, Alexander. *Two Models of Welfare: The Origins and Development of the Welfare State in Sweden and New Zealand, 1888–1988.* Publications of the Political Science Association in Uppsala, no. 108. Uppsala: Acta Universitatis Upsaliensis, 1989.

1472. Dohlman, Ebba. *National Welfare and Economic Interdependence: The Case of Sweden's Foreign Trade Policy.* Oxford: Clarendon Press; and New York: Oxford University Press, 1989.

1473. Pekkarinen, Jukka, Matti A. Pohjola, and Bob Rowthorn, eds. *Social Corporatism.* WIDER Studies in Development Economics. Oxford: Clarendon Press; and New York: Oxford University Press, 1992.

1474. Pontusson, Jonas. *The Limits of Social Democracy: Investment Politics in Sweden.* Cornell Studies in Political Economy. Ithaca: Cornell University Press, 1992.

Sweden—European Community Relations

1475. Lisein-Norman, Margaretha. *La Suede face à l'integration européenne.* Bruxelles: Institut d'études européennes, Université libre de Bruxelles, 1978.

1476. Viklund, Daniel. *Sweden and the European Community: Trade, Cooperation, and Policy Issues.* Uppsala: Swedish Institute, 1989.

Sweden—Foreign Relations

1477. Astrom, Sverker. *Sweden's Policy of Neutrality.* 3d ed. Stockholm: Swedish Institute, 1987.

1478. Carlgren, W. M. *Swedish Foreign Policy During the Second World War.* Translated by Arthur Spencer. New York: St. Martin's Press, 1977. Originally published as *Svensk utrikespolitik, 1939–1945.*

1479. Kennedy-Minott, Rodney. *Lonely Path to Follow: Nonaligned Sweden, United States/NATO, and the USSR.* Essays in Public Policy, no. 15. Stanford: Hoover Institution, 1990.

1480. Sundelius, Bengt. *The Committed Neutral: Sweden's Foreign Policy.* Westview Special Studies in International Relations. Boulder: Westview Press, 1989.

Sweden—History

1481. Andersson, Ingvar, and Jorgen Weibull. *Swedish History in Brief.* 2d ed. Stockholm: Swedish Institute, 1980.

1482. Scott, Franklin Daniel. *Sweden, the Nation's History.* Enl. ed. Carbondale: Southern Illinois University Press, 1988.

Sweden—Immigration

1483. Hammar, Tomas, and Kerstin Lindby. *Swedish Immigration Research: Introductory Survey and Annotated Bibliography.* Report (Swedish Commission on Immigration Research), no. 10. Stockholm: LiberForlag/Almanna forlaget, 1979.

1484. Sweden. Statens Invandrarvek. *Sweden, a General Introduction for Immigrants.* Translated by Roger G. Tanner. 2d ed. Norrkoping: Statens Invandrarverk, 1986. Originally published as *Sverige, en samhallsorientering for invandrare.*

Sweden—Language

1485. Eriksson, Anders. *Aspects of Swedish Speech Rhythm.* Gothenburg Monographs in Linguistics, no. 9. Gothenburg: Dept. of Linguistics, University of Goteborg, 1991.

1486. Holmes, Philip, and Ian Hinchliffe. *Swedish: A Comprehensive Grammar.* London and New York: Routledge, 1993.

Sweden—Literature

1487. Algulin, Ingemar. *A History of Swedish Literature.* Stockholm: Swedish Institute, 1989.

1488. Scobbie, Irene, ed. *Aspects of Modern Swedish Literature.* Series A: Scandinavian Literary History and Criticism, no. 2. Norwich: Norvik Press, 1988.

1489. Wastberg, Per, ed. *An Anthology of Modern Swedish Literature.* Anthologies—International P.E.N. Books, no. 11. Merrick, N.Y.: Cross-Cultural Communications, 1979.

Sweden—Music

1490. Cnattingius, Claes M. *Contemporary Swedish Music.* Translated by Claude Stephenson. Stockholm: Swedish Institute, 1973.

1491. Roth, Lena, ed. *Musical Life in Sweden.* Translated by Michael Johns. Stockholm: Swedish Institute, 1987.

Sweden—Politics and Government

1492. Hadenius, Stig. *Swedish Politics During the 20th Century.* Translated and adapted for a foreign public by Victor Kayfetz. 3d ed. Stockholm: Swedish Institute, 1990. Originally published as *Svensk politik under 1900-talet.*

1493. Misgeld, Klaus, Karl Molin, and Klas Amark, eds. *Creating Social Democracy: A Century of the Social Democratic Labor Party in Sweden*. Translated from the Swedish by Jan Teeland. University Park: Pennsylvania State University Press, 1992. Originally published as *Socialdemokratins samhalle*.

1494. Sainsbury, Diane. *Swedish Social Democratic Ideology and Electoral Politics, 1944–1948*. Stockholm Studies in Politics, no. 17. Stockholm: Almqvist & Wiksell International, 1980.

1495. Sjøblom, Gunnar. *The Role of Political Parties in Denmark and in Sweden, 1970–84*. Forskningsrapport, 1985/6. Copenhagen: Institute of Political Studies, University of Copenhagen, 1985.

1496. Sjøblom, Gunnar, and Nils Stjernquist. *Political Parties and Public Administration in Sweden*. Copenhagen: Institute of Political Studies, University of Copenhagen, 1986.

Sweden—Regional Planning

1497. Pass, David. *Vallingby and Farsta—From Idea to Reality: The Suburban Development Process in a Large Swedish City*. Stockholm: Statens institut for byggnadsforskning, 1969.

Sweden—Religion

1498. Stendahl, Brita K. *The Force of Tradition: A Case Study of Women Priests in Sweden*. Philadelphia: Fortress Press, 1985.

SWITZERLAND

Switzerland—Art

1499. Horat, Heinz. *1000 Years of Swiss Art*. New York: Huson Hills Press, 1992.

Switzerland—Economics

1500. Braillard, Philippe, Oleg Betcher, and Graziano Lusenti. *Switzerland as a Financial Center*. Translated by Ian Tickle. Dordrecht and Boston: Kluwer Academic Publishers, 1988. Originally published as *Place financière suisse*.

1501. Gunthardt, Walter, Robert Gnant, and Hans Erni. *Made in Switzerland: Synopsis of the Swiss Export Industry*. Translated by Stanley Mason. Zurich: A. Vetter, 1976.

1502. Widmer, Jean Philippe. *Le rôle de la main d'œuvre étrangère dans l'évolution du marché suisse du travail de 1945 à 1976*.

Neuchatel: Université de Neuchatel, Faculté de droit et des sciences économiques, 1978.

1503. Ziegler, Jean. *Switzerland Exposed.* Translated by Rosemary Sheed Middleton. London: Allison & Busby, 1978. Originally published as *Suisse au-dessus de tout soupçon.*

Switzerland — Ethnic Relations

1504. Bory, Valerie. *Dehors!: De la chasse aux Italiens à la peur des refugiés, 1896–1986.* Collection "En Suisse." Lausanne: P.-M. Favre, 1987.

1505. Ireland, Patrick Richard. *The Policy Challenge of Ethnic Diversity: Immigrant Politics in France and Switzerland.* Cambridge: Harvard University Press, 1994.

1506. Schmid, Carol L. *Conflict and Consensus in Switzerland.* Berkeley and London: University of California Press, 1981.

Switzerland — European Community Relations

1507. Du Bois, Pierre. *La Suisse et le Défi Européen: 1945–1992.* Lausanne: Favre, 1989.

1508. Weibel, Ewald R., and Markus Feller. *Schweizerische Identität und Europäische Integration.* Publikation der Akademischen Kommission der Universität Bern. Bern: Haupt, 1992.

Switzerland — Foreign Relations

1509. Huldt, Bo, and Atis Lejins, eds. *Neutrals in Europe: Switzerland.* Conference Papers (Swedish Institute of International Affairs), no. 10. Stockholm: The Institute, 1989.

1510. Meier, Heinz K. *Friendship Under Stress: U.S. Swiss Relations, 1900–1950.* Bern: Lang, 1970.

1511. Milivojević, Marko, and Pierre Maurer, eds. *Swiss Neutrality and Security.* New York: Berg, 1990.

1512. Probst, Raymond. *"Good Offices" in the Light of Swiss International Practice and Experience.* Dordrecht and Boston: M. Nijhoff, 1989.

Switzerland — Geography

1513. Barbier, Jacques, Jean-Luc Piveteau, and M. Roten. *Géographie de la Suisse.* Que sais-je? no. 1542. Paris: Presses universitaires de France, 1973.

Switzerland—History

1514. Bonjour, Edgar. *A Short History of Switzerland*. Oxford: Oxford University Press, 1952. Reprint. Westport, Conn.: Greenwood Press, 1985.

1515. Schwarz, Urs. *The Eye of the Hurricane: Switzerland in World War Two*. Boulder: Westview Press, 1980.

Switzerland—Language

1516. Heye, Jurgen B. *A Sociolinguistic Investigation of Multilingualism in the Canton of Ticino, Switzerland*. Janua linguarum: Series practica, 241. The Hague: Mouton, 1975.

Switzerland—Literature

1517. Flood, John L., ed. *Modern Swiss Literature*. New York: St. Martin's Press, 1985.

1518. Waidson, H. M., ed. *Anthology of Modern Swiss Literature*. New York: St. Martin's Press, 1984.

Switzerland—Music

1519. Brody, Elaine, and Claire Brook. *The Music Guide to Belgium, Luxembourg, Holland, and Switzerland*. New York: Dodd, Mead, 1977.

Switzerland—Politics and Government

1520. Katzenstein, Peter J. *Corporatism and Change: Austria, Switzerland, and the Politics of Industry*. Ithaca: Cornell University Press, 1984.

1521. Linder, Wolf. *Swiss Democracy: Possible Solutions to Conflict in Multicultural Societies*. Houndmills, Basingstoke: Macmillan; and New York: St. Martin's Press, 1994.

1522. Steiner, Jurg. *Amicable Agreement Versus Majority Rule: Conflict Resolution in Switzerland*. Translated by Asger Braendgaard and Barbard Braendgaard. Rev. and enl. ed. Chapel Hill: University of North Carolina Press, 1974. Originally published as *Gewaltlose Politik und Kulturelle Vielfalt*.

Switzerland—Religion

1523. Blanc, Olivier. *Catholiques et protestants dans le pays de Vaud*. Histoire et société, no. 13. Genève: Labor et Fides, 1986.

1524. Mayer, Kurt Bernd. *La population juive de Suisse à la lumière du recensement fédéral de 1970*. S.l.: Fédération suisse des communautés israélites, 1975.

TURKEY

Turkey—Art

1525. Akurgal, Ekrem, ed. *The Art and Architecture of Turkey*. New York: Rizzoli, 1980.

Turkey—Economics

1526. Eralp, Atila, Muharrem Tunay, and Birol Yesilada, eds. *The Political and Socioeconomic Transformation of Turkey*. Westport, Conn.: Praeger, 1993.

1527. Heper, Metin, ed. *Strong State and Economic Interest Groups: The Post-1980 Turkish Experience*. Berlin and New York: Walter de Gruyter, 1991.

1528. Onis, Ziya, and James Riedel. *Economic Crisis and Long-Term Growth in Turkey*. World Bank Comparative Macroeconomic Studies. Washington, D.C.: World Bank, 1993.

Turkey—European Community Relations

1529. Binark, Ismet, Erdogan Ozturk, and Ibrahim Karaer. *Turkey-European Community Bibliography: 1957–1990*. Ankara: T. C. Basbakanlik, Devlet Arsivleri Genel Mudurlugu, Dokumantasyon Dairesi Baskanligi, 1990.

1530. European Economic Community. *Agreement Setting up an Association Between the European Economic Community and Turkey*. London: H.M.S.O., 1966.

1531. European Economic Community. *EEC-Turkey Association Agreement and Protocols, and Other Basic Texts*. Luxembourg: Office for Official Publications of the European Communities, 1992.

1532. Gsanger, Hans. *Turkey-European Community: National Development Policy and the Process of Rapprochement*. Occasional Papers of the German Development Institute (GDI), no. 58. Berlin: German Development Institute, 1979.

1533. Korner, Heiko, and Rasul Shams. *Institutional Aspects of Economic Integration of Turkey into the European Community*. Hamburg: Verlag Weltarchiv, 1990.

Turkey—Foreign Relations

1534. Barchard, David. *Turkey and the West.* Chatham House Papers; no. 27. London and Boston: Published for the Royal Institute of International Affairs by Routledge & Kegan Paul, 1985.

1535. Campany, Richard C. *Turkey and the United States: The Arms Embargo Period.* New York: Praeger, 1986.

1536. Gianaris, Nicholas V. *Greece & Turkey.* New York: Praeger, 1988.

1537. Robins, Philip. *Turkey and the Middle East.* Chatham House Papers. New York: Council on Foreign Relations Press, 1991.

Turkey—History

1538. Browning, Janet. *Ataturk's Legacy to the Women of Turkey.* Durham: University of Durham, Center for Middle Eastern and Islamic Studies, 1985.

1539. Eralp, Atila, Muharrem Tunay, and Birol Yesilada, eds. *The Political and Socioeconomic Transformation of Turkey.* Westport, Conn.: Praeger, 1993.

1540. Heper, Metin. *Historical Dictionary of Turkey.* European Historical Dictionaries, no. 2. Metuchen, N.J.: Scarecrow Press, 1994.

1541. Lewis, Bernard. *The Emergence of Modern Turkey.* 2d ed. London and New York: Issued under the auspices of the Royal Institute of International Affairs by Oxford University Press, 1968.

1542. Nyrop, Richard F. *Turkey, a Country Study.* 3d ed. Area Handbook Series. Washington, D.C.: American University, 1980.

1543. Schick, Irvin Cemil, and Ertugrul Ahmet Tonak, eds. *Turkey in Transition.* New York: Oxford University Press, 1987.

Turkey—Language

1544. Boeschoten, Handrik, and Ludo Th. Verhoeven. *Turkish Linguistics Today.* New York: E. J. Brill, 1991.

1545. Menges, Karl Heinrich. *The Turkic Languages and Peoples.* Ural-altaische Bibliothek; 15. Wiesbaden: Harrassowitz, 1968.

Turkey—Literature

1546. Halman, Talat Sait. *Contemporary Turkish Literature.* Rutherford, N.J.: Fairleigh Dickinson University Press, 1982.

1547. Mitler, Louis. *Contemporary Turkish Writers.* Uralic and Altaic Series; no. 146. Bloomington: Indiana University, Research Institute for Inner Asian Studies, 1988.

1548. Riemann, Wolfgang. *Das Deutschlandbild in der modernen türkischen Literatur.* Wiesbaden: Harrassowitz, 1983.

1549. Stone, Frank A. *The Rub of Cultures in Modern Turkey: Literary Views of Education.* Uralic and Altaic Series, no. 123. Bloomington, Ind.: Indiana University, 1973.

Turkey—Migration

1550. Aker, Ahmet. *A Study of Turkish Labour Migration to Germany.* Discussion Paper, no. 10. Bologna: Institute of Foreign Policy Research, Bologna Center, Johns Hopkins University, 1974.

1551. Hansen, Bent. *Unemployment, Migration, and Wages in Turkey, 1962–85.* Policy, Planning, and Research Working Papers; 230. Washington, D.C.: World Bank, 1989.

1552. Krane, Ronald E. *Manpower Mobility Across Cultural Boundaries: Social, Economic, and Legal Aspects: The Case of Turkey and West Germany.* Social, Economic, and Political Studies of the Middle East; no. 16. Leiden: Brill, 1975.

1553. Martin, Philip L. *The Unfinished Story: Turkish Labour Migration to Western Europe: With Special Reference to the Federal Republic of Germany.* Geneva: ILO, 1991.

1554. Zimmermann, Klaus, ed. *Migration and Economic Development.* Regulation Economics. Berlin and New York: Springer-Verlag, 1992.

Turkey—Music

1555. Stokes, Martin. *The Arabesk Debate: Music and Musicians in Modern Turkey.* Oxford Studies in Social and Cultural Anthropology. New York: Oxford University Press, 1992.

Turkey—Politics and Government

1556. Ahmad, Feroz. *The Turkish Experiment in Democracy, 1950–1975.* London: C. Hurst for the Royal Institute of International Affairs, 1977.

1557. Bodurgil, Abraham. *Turkey, Politics and Government: A Bibliography, 1938–1975.* Washington, D.C.: Library of Congress, 1978.

1558. Geyikdagi, Mehmet Yasar. *Political Parties in Turkey: The Role of Islam*. New York: Praeger, 1984.

1559. Heper, Metin, and Ahmet Evin, eds. *Politics in the Third Turkish Republic*. Boulder: Westview Press, 1994.

1560. Heper, Metin, and Jacob M. Landau, eds. *Political Parties and Democracy in Turkey*. London and New York: I. B. Tauris, 1991.

1561. Onulduran, Ersin. *Political Development and Political Parties in Turkey*. Ankara Universitesi Siyasal Bilgiler Fakultesi Yayinlari, no. 370. Ankara: University of Ankara, Faculty of Political Science, 1974.

1562. Pevsner, Lucille W. *Turkey's Political Crisis*. Washington Papers; no. 110. New York: Praeger, 1984.

1563. Rustow, Dankwart A. *Turkey, America's Forgotten Ally*. New York: Council on Foreign Relations Press, 1989.

Turkey—Religion

1564. Galante, Abraham. *Histoire des juifs de Turquie*. 9 Vols. Istanbul: Isis, 1985.

1565. Marcus, Julie. *A World of Difference: Islam and Gender Hierarchy in Turkey*. Women in Asia Publication Series. London and Atlantic Highlands, N.J.: Zed, 1992.

1566. Papadopoullos, Theodoros. *Studies and Documents Relating to the History of the Greek Church and People Under Turkish Domination*. 2d ed. Aldershot, Hampshire, Variorum, and Brookfield, Vt.: Gower, 1990.

1567. Topper, Richard, ed. *Islam in Modern Turkey*. London and New York: I. B. Tauris, 1991.

THE VATICAN

1568. Daim, Wilfried. *The Vatican and Eastern Europe*. Translated by Alexander Gode. New York: Ungar, 1970. Originally published as *Vatikan und der Osten*.

1569. Ellis, Kail C., ed. *The Vatican, Islam, and the Middle East*. Contemporary Issues in the Middle East. Syracuse: Syracuse University Press, 1987.

1570. Gilbert, Arthur. *The Vatican Council and the Jews*. Cleveland: World Pub. Co., 1968.

1571. Gramick, Jeannine, and Pat Furey, eds. *The Vatican and Homosexuality*. New York: Crossroad, 1988.

1572. May, William W., ed. *Vatican Authority and American Catholic Dissent: The Curran Case and its Consequences*. New York: Crossroad, 1987.

1573. Pichon, Charles. *The Vatican and its Role in World Affairs*. Translated by Jean Misrahi. Westport, Conn.: Greenwood Press, 1969. Originally published as *Histoire du Vatican*.

1574. Zahn, Gordon Charles. *German Catholics and Hitler's Wars: A Study in Social Control*. New York: Sheed and Ward, 1962. Reprint. Notre Dame: University of Notre Dame Press, 1989.

WALES

Wales—Art

1575. Fifty-Six Group Wales. *The Artist and How to Employ Him*. Cardiff: 56 Group Wales, 1976.

1576. Rowan, Eric. *Art in Wales: An Illustrated History, 1850–1980*. Cardiff: Welsh Arts Council, University of Wales Press, 1985.

Wales—Economics

1577. George, K. D., and Lynn Mainwaring, eds. *The Welsh Economy*. Cardiff: University of Wales Press, 1988.

1578. Morris, Jonathan, and Stephen Hill. *Wales in the 1990s: A European Investment Region*. EIU European Investment Regions Series. New York: Economist Intelligence Unit, 1991.

Wales—Geography and Regional Planning

1579. Carter, Harold, and H. M. Griffiths, eds. *National Atlas of Wales*. Cardiff: Published by the University of Wales Press for the Social Science Committee, Board of Celtic Studies, University of Wales, 1989.

1580. Clavel, Pierre. *Opposition Planning in Wales and Appalachia*. Philadelphia: Temple University Press, 1983.

1581. Great Britain. Dept. of the Environment. *Town and Country Planning*. London: H.M.S.O., 1978.

Wales—History

1582. Jenkins, Philip. *A History of Modern Wales, 1536–1990*. London and New York: Longman, 1992.

1583. Mayo, Patricia Elton. *The Roots of Identity: Three National Movements in Contemporary European Politics*. London: Allen Lane, 1974.

1584. Morgan, Kenneth O. *Rebirth of a Nation: Wales, 1880–1980*. The History of Wales, v. 6. New York: Oxford University Press, 1981.

Wales—Language

1585. Khleif, Bud B. *Language, Ethnicity, and Education in Wales*. Contributions to the Sociology of Language, no. 28. The Hague and New York: Mouton, 1980.

Wales—Literature

1586. Dale-Jones, Don, and Randal Jenkins, eds. *Twelve Modern Anglo-Welsh Poets*. London: University of London Press, 1975.

1587. Handley-Taylor, Geoffrey, ed. *Authors of Wales Today*. Country Authors Today Series. London: Eddison Press, 1972.

1588. *Location Register of Twentieth-Century English Literary Manuscripts and Letters: A Union List of Papers of Modern English, Irish, Scottish, and Welsh Authors in the British Isles*. 2 vols. Boston: G. K. Hall, 1988.

1589. Osmond, John. *The Future of the Word*. Mumbles, Swansea: Welsh Union of Writers, 1985.

Wales—Migration

1590. Great Britain. Welsh Office. *Migration Into, Out Of, and Within Wales in the 1966–71 Period*. Welsh Office Occasional Paper, no. 4. Cardiff: Welsh Office, Economic Services Division, 1979.

Wales—Music

1591. Brody, Elaine, and Claire Brook. *The Music Guide to Great Britain: England, Scotland, Wales, Ireland*. New York: Dodd, Mead, 1975.

1592. Gwynn Williams, and William Sidney. *Welsh National Music and Dance*. 4th ed. Llangollen: Gwynn Pub. Co., 1971.

Wales—Politics and Government

1593. Adamson, David L. *Class, Ideology, and the Nation: A Theory of Welsh Nationalism*. Cardiff: University of Wales Press, 1991.

1594. Davies, Charlotte Aull. *Welsh Nationalism in the Twentieth Century*. New York: Praeger, 1989.

1595. Philip, Alan Butt. *The Welsh Question: Nationalism in Welsh Politics, 1945–1970*. Cardiff: University of Wales Press, 1975.

Wales—Religion

1596. Davies, D. Elwyn. *"They Thought for Themselves": A Brief Look at the Story of Unitarianism and the Liberal Tradition in Wales and Beyond its Borders*. Llandysul: Gomer Press, 1982.

Famous People

Famous People—Adenauer, Konrad (1876–1967)

1597. Adenauer, Konrad. *Memoirs, 1945–1953*. Translated by Beate Ruhm von Oppen. London: Weidenfeld & Nicholson, 1966. Originally published as *Erinnerungen*.

1598. Hildebrand, Klaus. *German Foreign Policy from Bismarck to Adenauer: The Limits of Statecraft*. Translated by Louise Willmot. London and Boston: Unwin Hyman, 1989. Originally published as *Staatskunst oder Systemzwang*.

1599. Hiscocks, Richard. *The Adenauer Era*. Philadelphia: Lippincott, 1966.

1600. McGhee, George Crews. *At the Creation of a New Germany: From Adenauer to Brandt: An Ambassador's Account*. New Haven: Yale University Press, 1989.

Famous People—Attlee, Clement Richard (1883–1967)

1601. Harris, Kenneth. *Attlee*. London: Weidenfeld and Nicolson, 1982.

1602. Morgan, Kenneth O. *Labour in Power, 1945–1951*. Oxford and New York: Oxford University Press, 1985.

1603. Pearce, Robert D. *Attlee's Labour Government, 1945–51*. Lancaster Pamphlet. London and New York: Routledge, 1994.

Famous People—Brandt, Willy (1913–)

1604. Brandt, Willy. *In Exile: Essays, Reflections and Letters, 1933–1947*. Translated by R. W. Last. London: Wolff, 1971. Originally published as *Draussen*.

1605. Brandt, Willy. *My Life in Politics*. London and New York: Hamish Hamilton, 1992. Originally published as *Erinnerungen*.

1606. Brandt, Willy. *People and Politics: The Years 1960–1975.* Translated by J. Maxwell Brownjohn. London: Collins, 1978. Originally published as *Begegnungen und Einsichten.*

1607. Fletcher, Roger, ed. *Bernstein to Brandt: A Short History of German Social Democracy.* London: Edward Arnold, 1987.

1608. Whetten, Lawrence L. *Germany's Ostpolitik: Relations between the Federal Republic and the Warsaw Pact Countries.* Oxford Paperbacks, no. 26. London and New York: Oxford University Press for the Royal Institute of International Affairs, 1971.

Famous People—Cassin, René (1887–1976)

1609. Agi, Marc, *De l'idée d'universalité comme fondatrice du concept des droits de l'homme d'après la vie et l'œuvre de René Cassin.* Antibes: Alp'Azur, 1980.

1610. Agi, Marc. *René Cassin: fantassin des droits de l'homme.* Paris: Plon, 1979.

1611. Israel, Gerard. *René Cassin, 1887–1976: Le guerre hors la loi, avec de Gaulle, les droits de l'homme.* Collection "Prophètes pour demain." Paris: Desclée de Brouwer, 1990.

1612. Newman, Ralph Abraham, ed. *Equity in the World's Legal Systems: A Comparative Study, Dedicated to René Cassin.* Studies in Jurisprudence, no. 1. Brussels: E. Bruylant, 1973.

Famous People—Chirac, Jacques (1932–)

1613. Giesbert, Franz-Olivier. *Jacques Chirac.* Paris: Seuil, 1987,

1614. Tuppen, John N. *Chirac's France, 1986–88: Contemporary Issues in French Society.* New York: St. Martin's Press, 1991.

Famous People—Churchill, Winston, Sir (1874–1965)

1615. Charmley, John. *Churchill, the End of Glory: A Political Biography.* 1st U.S. ed. New York: Harcourt Brace, 1993.

1616. Churchill, Winston. *A History of the English-Speaking Peoples.* 4 vols. New York: Dodd Mead, 1956–1958.

1617. Churchill, Winston. *The Boer War.* 1st American ed. New York: W. W. Norton, 1990.

1618. Churchill, Winston. *Great Contemporaries.* 1st American ed. New York: Norton, 1991.

1619. Churchill, Winston. *Memoirs of the Second World War*. Boston: Houghton Mifflin, 1990. Abridgement of the *Second World War*.

1620. Churchill, Winston. *The Second World War*. 6 vols. Boston: Houghton Mifflin, 1985–1986.

1621. Churchill, Winston. *The World Crisis*. New York: Scribner; and Toronto: Maxwell Macmillan Canada, 1992. Abridgement of the *History of World War I*.

1622. Churchill, Winston, and Dwight D. Eisenhower. *The Churchill-Eisenhower Correspondence, 1953–1955*. Chapel Hill: University of North Carolina Press, 1990.

1623. Churchill, Winston, and Franklin D. Roosevelt. *Churchill & Roosevelt: The Complete Correspondence*. 3 vols. Princeton: Princeton University Press, 1984.

1624. Cohen, Ronald I. *A Bibliography of the Works of Sir Winston Churchill*. Forthcoming.

1625. Jablonsky, David. *Churchill, the Making of a Grand Strategist*. Carlisle Barracks, Pa.: Strategic Studies Institute, U.S. Army War College, 1990.

1626. Lawlor, Sheila. *Churchill and the Politics of War, 1940–1941*. Cambridge and New York: Cambridge University Press, 1994.

1627. Mayer, Frank A. *The Opposition Years: Winston S. Churchill and the Conservative Party, 1945–1951*. American University Studies. Series IX History, no. 116. New York: P. Lang, 1992.

1628. Sainsbury, Keith. *Churchill and Roosevelt at War: The War They Fought and the Peace They Hoped to Make*. New York: New York University Press, 1994.

1629. Young, John W., ed. *The Foreign Policy of Churchill's Peacetime Administration, 1951–1955*. Leicester: Leicester University Press, 1988.

Famous People—Craxi, Bettino (1934–)

1630. Craxi, Bettino. *Cresce l'Italia*. Il Cielo della politica. Milan: SugarCo, 1987.

1631. Craxi, Bettino. *L'Italia liberata*. Milan: SugarCo, 1984.

1632. Craxi, Bettino. *Il progresso italiano*. 2d ed. 2 vols. Milano: SugarCo, 1985-1989.

Famous People—De Beauvoir, Simone (1908–1986)

1633. Bennett, Joy, and Gabriella Hochmann. *Simone de Beauvoir: An Annotated Bibliography*. Garland Reference Library of the Humanities, no. 774. New York: Garland, 1988.

1634. De Beauvoir, Simone. *Adieux: A Farewell to Sartre*. Translated by Patrick O'Brian. 1st American ed. New York: Pantheon Books, 1984. Originally published as *Cérémonie des adieux*.

1635. De Beauvoir, Simone. *All Said and Done*. Translated by Patrick O'Brian. Introduction by Toril Moi. 1st Paragon House ed. New York: Paragon House, 1993. Originally published as *Toute compte fait*.

1636. De Beauvoir, Simone. *Letters to Sartre*. Translated and edited by Quintin Hoare. London: Radius, 1991. Originally published as *Lettres à Sartre*.

1637. De Beauvoir, Simone. *The Prime of Life*. Translated by Peter Green. 1st Paragon ed. New York: Paragon House, 1992. Originally published as *La Force de l'âge*.

1638. Francis, Claude, and Fernande Gontier. *Les écrits de Simone de Beauvoir: La vie, l'écriture, avec en appendice, textes inédits ou retrouvés*. Paris: Gallimard, 1979.

1639. Keefe, Terry. *French Existentialist Fiction: Changing Moral Perspectives*. Totowa, N.J.: Barnes & Noble, 1986.

1640. Moi, Toril. *Feminist Theory & Simone de Beauvoir*. The Bucknell Lectures in Literary Theory, no. 3. Oxford and Cambridge, Mass.: Blackwell, 1990.

1641. Moi, Toril. *Simone de Beauvoir: The Making of an Intellectual Woman*. Oxford and Cambridge, Mass.: Blackwell, 1994.

1642. Peters, Helene. *The Existential Women*. American University Studies. Series XXVII, Feminist Studies, no. 3. New York: P. Lang, 1990.

1643. Sartre, Jean-Paul. *Witness to my Life: The Letters of Jean-Paul Sartre to Simone de Beauvoir, 1926–1939*. Translated by Lee Fahnestock and Norman McAfee. New York: Scribner's, 1993. Originally published as *Lettres au Castor et à quelques autres*.

1644. Simons, Margaret A. *Feminist Interpretations of Simone de Beauvoir*. Re-reading the Canon. University Park: Pennsylvania State University Press, 1995.

Famous People—De Gasperi, Alcide (1881–1954)

1645. Arnoulx de Pirey, Elisabeth. *De Gasperi: le père italien de l'Europe*. Paris: P. Tequi, 1991.

1646. Keyserlingk, Robert Wendelin. *Patriots of Peace*. Gerrards Cross: Smythe, 1972.

1647. Scoppola, Pietro. *La proposta politica di De Gasperi*. 2d ed. Bologne: Mulino, 1978.

1648. Valiani, Leo. *L'Italia di De Gasperi, 1945–1954*. Quaderni di storia, no. 56. Florence: F. Le Monnier, 1982.

Famous People—De Gaulle, Charles (1890–1970)

1649. Berstein, Serge. *The Republic of De Gaulle, 1958–1969*. Translated by Peter Morris. The Cambridge History of Modern France, no. 8. Cambridge and New York: Cambridge University Press, 1993. Originally published as *France de l'expansion*.

1650. Cerny, Philip G. *The Politics of Grandeur: Ideological Aspects of De Gaulle's Foreign Policy*. Cambridge and New York: Cambridge University Press, 1980.

1651. De Gaulle, Charles. *The Army of the Future*. Philadelphia: Lippincott, 1941. Reprint. Westport, Conn.: Greenwood Press, 1976. Originally published as *Vers l'armée de métier*.

1652. De Gaulle, Charles. *The Complete War Memoirs of Charles de Gaulle, 1940–1946*. New York: Da Capo Press, 1984. Originally published as: *Mémoires de guerre*.

1653. De Gaulle, Charles. *The Edge of the Sword*. Westport, Conn.: Greenwood Press, 1975. Originally published as *Fil de l'épée*.

1654. Debray, Regis. *Charles de Gaulle, Existentialist of the Nation*. Translated by John Howe. London and New York: Verso, 1994. Originally published as *A demain de Gaulle*.

1655. Debré, Jean Louis. *Les idées constitutionnelles du général de Gaulle*. Bibliothèque constitutionnelle et de science politique, no. 49. Paris: Librairie générale de droit et de jurisprudence, 1974.

1656. De Porte, Anton W. *De Gaulle's Foreign Policy, 1944–1946*. Cambridge: Harvard University Press, 1968.

1657. Furniss, Edgar Stephenson. *France, Troubled Ally: De Gaulle's Heritage and Prospects*. Westport, Conn.: Greenwood Press, 1974.

1658. Gordon, Philip H. *A Certain Idea of France: French Security Policy and the Gaullist Legacy.* Princeton Studies in International History and Politics. Princeton: Princeton University Press, 1993.

1659. Gough, Hugh, and John Horne, eds. *De Gaulle and Twentieth-Century France.* London and New York: Edward Arnold, 1994.

1660. Hostache, Rene. *Le général de Gaulle, Jean Moulin et la création du C.N.R.* Paris: Editions La Bruyère, 1989.

1661. Kristeva, Julia. *Nations Without Nationalism.* Translated by Leon S. Roudiez. European Perspectives. New York: Columbia University Press, 1993. Originally published as *Lettre ouverte à Harlem Desir.*

1662. Lacouture, Jean. *De Gaulle.* 1st American ed. 2 vols. New York: Norton, 1990–1992.

1663. Thompson, Robert Smith. *Pledge to Destiny: Charles de Gaulle and the Rise of the Free French.* New York: McGraw-Hill, 1974.

1664. White, Dorothy Shipley. *Black Africa and De Gaulle From the French Empire to Independence.* University Park: Pennsylvania State University Press, 1979.

Famous People — Delors, Jacques (1925–)

1665. Bodman, Eric de, and Bertrand Richard. *Changer les relations sociales: La politique de Jacques Delors.* Collections Relations Industrielles. Paris: Editions d'organisation, 1976.

1666. Delors, Jacques. *Our Europe: The Community and National Development.* Translated by Brian Pearce. London and New York: Verso, 1992. Originally published as *France par l'Europe.*

1667. Delors, Jacques, and Claude Glayman. *Changer: Conversations avec Claude Glayman.* Les Grands Leaders. Paris: Stock, 1975.

Famous People — Elizabeth II, Queen of the United Kingdom (1926–)

1668. Howard, Philip. *The British Monarchy in the Twentieth Century.* London: Hamilton, 1977.

1669. Levine, Gemma. *Gemma Levine's Faces of the 80s.* Foreword by Margaret Thatcher. London: Collins Publishers, 1987.

1670. Longford, Elizabeth. *The Queen: The Life of Elizabeth II.* 1st U.S. ed. New York: Knopf, 1983.

1671. McDonald, Trevor, and Peter Tiffin. *The Queen and the Commonwealth.* London: Thames: Methuen, 1986.

1672. Vickers, Hugo. *We Want the Queen*. London: Debrett's Peerage Ltd., 1977.

Famous People—Franco, Francisco (1892–1975)

1673. Ellwood, Sheelagh M. *Franco*. Profiles in Power. London and New York: Longman, 1994.

1674. Fusi Aizpurua, Juan Pablo. *Franco: A Biography*. Translated by Felipe Fernandez-Armesto. 1st U.S. ed. New York: Harper & Row, 1987. Originally published as Franco: *Autoritarismo y Poder Personal*.

1675. Hansen, Edward C. *Rural Catalonia Under the Franco Regime: The Fate of Regional Culture Since the Spanish Civil War*. Cambridge and New York: Cambridge University Press, 1977.

1676. Higginbotham, Virginia. *Spanish Film Under Franco*. Austin: University of Texas Press, 1988.

1677. Payne, Stanley G. *The Franco Regime, 1936–1975*. Madison: University of Wisconsin Press, 1987.

Famous People—George VI, King of the United Kingdom (1895–1952)

1678. Aronson, Theo. *The Royal Family at War*. London: John Murray, 1993.

1679. Bradford, Sarah. *King George VI*. London: Weidenfeld and Nicolson, 1989.

1680. Morris, James. *Farewell the Trumpets: An Imperial Retreat*. 1st Harvest/HBJ ed. New York: Harcourt Brace Jovanovich, 1980.

1681. Raghunathrao Shankarrao, Sir, Raja of Bhor. *Royal Coronation and My Second Trip to Europe, 1937*. Bhor: L. R. Sane, 1942.

1682. Sinclair, David. *Two Georges: The Making of the Modern Monarchy*. London: Hodder and Stoughton, 1988.

1683. Townsend, Peter. *The Last Emperor, An Intimate Account of George VI and the Fall of His Empire*. New York: Simon and Schuster, 1976.

Famous People—Giscard d'Estaing, Valery (1926–)

1684. Bassi, Michel. *Valery Giscard d'Estaing*. Paris: B. Grosset, 1968.

1685. Frears, John R. *France in the Giscard Presidency*. London and Boston: G. Allen & Unwin, 1981.

1686. Wright, Vincent, ed. *Continuity and Change in France*. London and Boston: G. Allen & Unwin, 1984.

Famous People—Hammarskjold, Dag (1905–1961)

1687. Beskow, Bo. *Dag Hammarskjold: Strictly Personal; A Portrait.* Garden City, N.Y.: Doubleday, 1969.

Famous People—Hitler, Adolf (1889–1945)

1688. Abel, Theodore Fred. *Why Hitler Came into Power.* New York: Prentice-Hall, 1938. Reprint. Cambridge: Harvard University Press, 1986.

1689. Barnes, James J., and Patience P. Barnes. *Hitler's Mein Kampf in Britain and America: A Publishing History, 1930–39.* Cambridge and New York: Cambridge University Press, 1980.

1690. Barnett, Correlli, ed. *Hitler's Generals.* London: Weidenfeld and Nicolson, 1989.

1691. Broszat, Martin. *The Hitler State: The Foundation and Development of the Internal Structure of the Third Reich.* Translated by John W. Hiden. London and New York: Longman, 1981. Originally published as *Staat Hitlers.*

1692. Bullock, Alan. *Hitler and Stalin: Parallel Lives.* 1st American ed. New York: Knopf, 1992.

1693. Fleming, Gerald. *Hitler and the Final Solution.* Berkeley: University of California Press, 1984. Originally published as *Hitler und die Endlösung.*

1694. Flood, Charles Bracelen. *Hitler, the Path to Power.* Boston: Houghton Mifflin, 1989.

1695. Gordon, Sarah Ann. *Hitler, Germans, and the "Jewish Question."* Princeton: Princeton University Press, 1984.

1696. Hamilton, Charles. *The Hitler Diaries: Fakes that Fooled the World.* Lexington: University Press of Kentucky, 1991.

1697. Hitler, Adolf. *Hitler's Table Talk, 1941–44: His Private Conversations.* Translated by Norman Cameron and R. H. Stevens. 2d ed. London: Weidenfeld and Nicolson, 1973. Originally published as *Bormann-Vermerke.*

1698. Hitler, Adolf. *Mein Kampf.* Editorial sponsors: John Chamberlain, Sidney B. Fay . . . New York: Reynal & Hitchcock, 1939.

1699. Hitler, Adolf. *Mein Kampf.* Translated by Ralph Manheim. London: Hutchinson, 1969.

1700. Hitler, Adolf. *The Speeches of Adolf Hitler, April 1922-August 1939: An English Translation of Representative Passages.*

Arranged under Subjects and Edited by Norman H. Baynes. Reprint of the 1942 ed. 2 vols. New York: H. Fertig, 1969.

1701. Hoffmann, Peter. *German Resistance to Hitler.* Cambridge: Harvard University Press, 1988. Originally published as *Widerstand gegen Hitler.*

1702. Jablonsky, David. *Strategic Rationality Is Not Enough: Hitler and the Concept of Crazy States.* Professional Readings in Military Strategy, no. 3. Carlisle Barracks, Pa.: Strategic Studies Institute, U.S. Army War College, 1991.

1703. Jenks, William Alexander. *Vienna and the Young Hitler.* New York: Columbia University Press, 1960.

1704. Koch, Hannsjoachim Wolfgang, ed. *Aspects of the Third Reich.* New York: St. Martin's Press, 1985.

1705. Maser, Werner. *Hitler's Letters and Notes.* Translated by Arnold Pomerans. 1st U.S. ed. New York: Harper & Row, 1974. Originally published as *Hitlers Briefe und Notizen.*

1706. Nicholls, Anthony James. *Weimar and the Rise of Hitler.* 3d ed. The Making of the 20th century. New York: St. Martin's Press, 1991.

1707. Rhodes, James M. *The Hitler Movement: A Modern Millenarian Revolution.* Hoover Institution Publication, no. 213. Stanford: Hoover Institution Press, 1980.

1708. Rosenfeld, Alvin Hirsch. *Imagining Hitler.* Bloomington: Indiana University Press, 1985.

1709. Schwaab, Edleff H. *Hitler's Mind: A Plunge into Madness.* New York: Praeger, 1992.

1710. Shirer, William L. *The Rise and Fall of the Third Reich: A History of Nazi Germany.* New York: Fawcett Crest, 1992.

1711. Simpson, William. *Hitler and Germany.* Cambridge Topics in History: Cambridge and New York: Cambridge University Press, 1991.

1712. Staudinger, Hans. *The Inner Nazi: A Critical Analysis of Mein Kampf.* Baton Rouge: Louisiana State University Press, 1981.

1713. Whealey, Robert H. *Hitler and Spain: The Nazi Role in the Spanish Civil War, 1936–1939.* Lexington: University Press of Kentucky, 1989.

1714. Wistrich, Robert S. *Hitler's Apocalypse: Jews and the Nazi Legacy.* 1st U.S. ed. New York: St. Martin's Press, 1985.

1715. Zalampas, Michael. *Adolf Hitler and the Third Reich in American Magazines, 1923–1939*. Bowling Green, Ohio: Bowling Green State University Popular Press, 1989.

Famous People—Honecker, Erich (1912–)

1716. Barnett, Thomas P. M. *Romanian and East German Policies in the Third World: Comparing the Strategies of Ceausescu and Honecker*. Westport, Conn.: Praeger, 1992.

1717. Childs, David, ed. *Honecker's Germany*. London and Boston: Allen & Unwin, 1985.

1718. Honecker, Erich. *From My Life*. Leaders of the World. Oxford and New York: Pergamon, 1981. Originally published as *Aus meinem Leben*.

1719. Ulbricht, Walter, Willi Stoph, and Erich Honecker. *The German Democratic Republic at the Beginning of Its Third Decade*. Dresden: Verlag Zeit im Bild, 1969.

Famous People—John XXIII, Pope (1881–1963)

1720. Bianchi, Eugene C. *John XXIII and American Protestants*. Washington: Corpus Books, 1968.

1721. Gorresio, Vittorio. *The New Mission of Pope John XXIII*. Translated by Charles Lam Markmann. New York: Funk & Wagnalls, 1970. Originally published as *La nuova missione*.

1722. Hebblethwaite, Peter. *John XXIII, Pope of the Council*. London: G. Chapman, 1984.

1723. Wynn, Wilton. *Keepers of the Keys: John XXIII, Paul VI, and John Paul II, three who changed the Church*. New York: Random House, 1988.

Famous People—John Paul II, Pope (1920–)

1724. Blazynski, George. *John Paul II: A Man From Kraków*. London: Weidenfeld and Nicolson, 1979.

1725. Hebblethwaite, Peter, and Ludwig Kaufmann. *John Paul II: A Pictorial Biography*. New York: McGraw-Hill, 1979.

Famous People—Juan Carlos I, King of Spain (1938–)

1726. Nourry, Philippe. *Juan Carlos, un roi pour les républicains*. 2e éd. Paris: Le Centurion, 1986.

1727. Uboldi, Raffaelo. *Juan Carlos*. Milan: Rizzoli, 1985.

Famous People—Kohl, Helmut (1930–)

1728. Derbyshire, Ian. *Politics in West Germany: From Schmidt to Kohl.* Chambers Political Spotlights. Edinburgh: Chambers, 1987.

1729. Kohl, Helmut. *History's Inescapable Impact on the Present.* Bonn: Press and Information Office of the Federal Govt., 1988.

1730. Maser, Werner. *Helmut Kohl: Der deutsche Kanzler: Biographie.* 2. Aufl. Frankfurt am Main: Ullstein, 1990.

1731. Muchler, Gunter, and Klaus Hofmann. *Helmut Kohl, Chancellor of German Unity: A Biography.* Translated by Kathleen-Muller Rostin. Bonn: Press and Information Office of the Federal Govt., 1992.

Famous People—Lemass, Sean (1899–1971)

1732. Bew, Paul, and Henry Patterson. *Sean Lemass and the Making of Modern Ireland, 1945–66.* Dublin: Gill and Macmillan, 1982.

1733. Farrell, Brian. *Sean Lemass.* Gill's Irish Lives. Dublin: Gill and Macmillan, 1983.

Famous People—Macmillan, Harold (1894–1986)

1734. Horne, Alistair. *Macmillan.* 2 vols. London: Macmillan, 1988–1989.

1735. Macmillan, Harold. *The Middle Way: A Study of the Problem of Economic and Social Progress in a Free and Democratic Society.* 1st ed. reissued with 'The Middle Way: 20 Years After'. London: Macmillan; and New York: St. Martin's Press, 1966.

1736. Macmillan, Harold. *War Diaries: Politics and War in the Mediterranean, January 1943–May 1945.* 1st U.S. ed. New York: St. Martin's Press, 1984.

1737. Sampson, Anthony. *Macmillan: A Study in Ambiguity.* New York: Simon and Schuster, 1967.

Famous People—Major, John (1943–)

1738. Anderson, Bruce. *John Major: The Making of the Prime Minister.* London: Fourth Estate, 1991.

1739. Pearce, Edward. *The Quiet Rise of John Major.* London: Weidenfeld and Nicolson, 1991.

Famous People—Mitterrand, François (1916–1996)

1740. Péan, Pierre. *Une jeunesse française: François Mitterrand, 1934–1947*. Paris: Fayard, 1994.

1741. Ross, George, Stanley Hoffmann, and Sylvia Malzacher, eds. *The Mitterrand Experiment: Continuity and Change in Modern France*. Europe and the International Order. New York: Oxford University Press, 1987.

1742. Singer, Daniel. *Is Socialism Doomed?: The Meaning of Mitterrand*. New York: Oxford University Press, 1988.

1743. Williams, Stuart. *Socialism in France: From Jaures to Mitterrand*. New York: St. Martin's Press, 1983.

Famous People—Monnet, Jean (1888–1979)

1744. Brinkley, Douglas, and Clifford Hackett, eds. *Jean Monnet: The Path to European Unity*. New York: St. Martin's Press, 1991.

1745. Bromberger, Merry, and Serge Bromberger. *Jean Monnet and the United States of Europe*. Translated by Elaine P. Halperin. New York: Coward-McCann, 1969. Originally published as *Les Coulisses de l'Europe*.

1746. Duchène, François. *Jean Monnet: The First Statesman of Interdependence*. New York: Norton, 1994.

1747. Fontaine, Pascal. *Jean Monnet: l'inspirateur*. Préface de Jacques Delors. Paris: J. Grancher, 1988.

1748. Giles, Frank. *The Locust Years: The Story of the Fourth Republic, 1946–1958*. New York: Carroll & Graf, 1994.

1749. Monnet, Jean. *Memoirs*. Translated by Richard Mayne. London: Collins, 1978. Originally published as *Mémoires*.

1750. *Témoignages à la mémoire de Jean Monnet*. Lausanne: Fondation Jean Monnet pour l'Europe, Centre de recherches européennes, 1989.

Famous People—Moro, Aldo (1916–1978)

1751. Jamieson, Alison. *The Heart Attacked: Terrorism and Conflict in the Italian State*. London; New York: M. Boyars, 1989.

1752. Wagner-Pacifici, Robin Erica. *The Moro Morality Play: Terrorism as Social Drama*. Chicago: University of Chicago Press, 1986.

Famous People—Mussolini, Benito (1883–1945)

1753. De Felice, Renzo. *Interpretations of Fascism.* Cambridge: Harvard University Press, 1977.

1754. Deakin, Frederick William. *The Brutal Friendship.* Garden City, N.Y.: Anchor Books, 1966.

1755. Diggins, John P. *Mussolini and Fascism: The View From America.* Princeton: Princeton University Press, 1972.

1756. Gallo, Max. *Mussolini's Italy: Twenty Years of the Fascist Era.* New York: Macmillan, 1973.

1757. Hoyt, Edwin Palmer. *Mussolini's Empire: The Rise and Fall of the Fascist Vision.* New York: J. Wiley, 1994.

Famous People—Paisley, Ian (1926–)

1758. Bruce, Steve. *God Save Ulster: The Religion and Politics of Paisleyism.* Oxford: Clarendon Press and New York: Oxford University Press, 1986.

1759. Smyth, Clifford. *Ian Paisley: Voice of Protestant Ulster.* Edinburgh: Scottish Academic, 1987.

Famous People—Palme, Olof (1927–1986)

1760. Mosey, Chris. *Cruel Awakening: Sweden and the Killing of Olof Palme.* London: Hurst and New York: St. Martin's Press, 1991.

Famous People—Pétain, Philippe (1856–1951)

1761. Griffiths, Richard. *Pétain; a Biography of Marshal Philippe Pétain of Vichy.* 1st U.S. ed. Garden City, N.Y.: Doubleday, 1972. Originally published as *Marshal Pétain.*

1762. Michel, Henri. *Pétain, Laval, Darlan, trois politiques?* Paris: Flammarion, 1972.

1763. Rousso, Henry. *The Vichy Syndrome: History and Memory in France Since 1944.* Translated by Arthur Goldhammer. Cambridge: Harvard University Press, 1991. Originally published as *Syndrome de Vichy.*

1764. Roy, Jules. *The Trial of Marshal Pétain.* Translated by Robert Baldick. 1st U.S. ed. New York: Harper & Row, 1967. Originally published as *Le grand naufrage.*

Famous People—Pius XII, Pope (1876–1958)

1765. Falconi, Carlo. *The Silence of Pius XII*. Translated by Bernard Wall. 1st American ed. Boston: Little, Brown, 1970. Originally published as *Il silenzio di Pio XII*.

1766. McGurn, Barrett. *A Reporter Looks at the Vatican*. New York: Coward-McCann, 1962.

1767. Rhodes, Anthony. *The Vatican in the Age of the Dictators, 1922–1945*. New York: Holt, Rinehart and Winston, 1974.

1768. Roosevelt, Franklin Delano, and Pius XII, Pope. *Wartime Correspondence Between President Roosevelt and Pope Pius XII*. President Franklin D. Roosevelt and the Era of the New Deal. New York: Da Capo Press, 1975.

Famous People—Pompidou, Georges (1911–1974)

1769. Alexandre, Philippe. *The Duel: De Gaulle and Pompidou*. Translated by Elaine P. Halperin. Boston: Houghton Mifflin, 1972. Originally published as *Duel: De Gaulle—Pompidou*.

1770. Debbasch, Charles. *La France de Pompidou*. Paris: Presses universitaires de France, 1974.

1771. Rials, Stephane. *Les idées politiques du président Georges Pompidou*. Travaux et recherches de l'Université de droit, d'économie et de sciences sociales de Paris: Série Science Politique; no. 9. Paris: Presses universitaires de France, 1977.

Famous People—Quisling, Vidkun (1887–1945)

1772. Hayes, Paul M. *Quisling: the Career and Political Ideas of Vidkun Quisling, 1887–1945*. Bloomington: Indiana University Press, 1972.

1773. Hoidal, Oddvar K. *Quisling: A Study in Treason* Oslo: Norwegian University Press, 1989.

Famous People—Salazar, António de Oliveira (1889–1970)

1774. Raby, David L. *Fascism and Resistance in Portugal: Communists, Liberals, and Military Dissidents in the Opposition to Salazar, 1941–1974*. Manchester, England, and New York: Manchester University Press, 1988.

Famous People — Schuman, Robert (1886–1963)

1775. Acheson, Dean. *Sketches From Life of Men I Have Known*. New York: Harper, 1961. Reprint. Westport, Conn.: Greenwood Press, 1974.

1776. Fontaine, Pascal. *Europe, a Fresh Start: The Schuman Declaration, 1950–90*. Luxembourg: Office for Official Publications of the European Communities, 1990.

1777. Poidevin, Raymond. *Robert Schuman: homme d'État, 1886–1963*. Paris: Impr. nationale, 1986.

Famous People — Schuschnigg, Kurt (1897–1977)

1778. Schuschnigg, Kurt. *The Brutal Takeover: The Austrian Ex-Chancellor's Account of the Anschluss of Austria by Hitler*. Translated by Richard Perry. London: Weidenfeld and Nicolson, 1971. Originally published as *Im Kampf gegen Hitler*.

Famous People — Soares, Mario (1924–)

1779. Janitschek, Hans. *Mario Soares: Portrait of a Hero*. New York: St. Martin's Press, 1986.

Famous People — Spaak, Paul Henri (1899–1972)

1780. Huizinga, Jakob Herman. *Mr. Europe*. New York: Praeger, 1961.

1781. Spaak, Paul-Henri. *Combats inachevés*. 2 vols. Paris: Fayard, 1969.

Famous People — Spinelli, Altiero (1907–1986)

1782. Levi, Lucio, ed. *Altiero Spinelli and Federalism in Europe and the World*. London: Lothian Foundation, 1991.

1783. Spinelli, Altiero. *Diario europeo*. 3 vols. Bologna: Il Mulino, 1989–1992.

1784. Spinelli, Altiero. *The Eurocrats: Conflict and Crisis in the European Community*. Translated by C. Grove Haines. Baltimore: Johns Hopkins University Press, 1966. Originally published as *Rapporto sull'Europa*.

Famous People — Thatcher, Margaret (1925–)

1785. Byrd, Peter, ed. *British Foreign Policy Under Thatcher*. Oxford: P. Allan; and New York: St. Martin's Press, 1988.

1786. Cosgrove, Patrick. *Margaret Thatcher: A Tory and Her Party*. London: Hutchinson, 1978.

1787. Johnson, Christopher. *The Economy Under Mrs. Thatcher, 1979–1990*. London and New York: Penguin Books, 1991.

1788. Kavanagh, Dennis. *Thatcherism and British Politics: The End of Consensus?* 2d ed. New York: Oxford University Press, 1990.

1789. Riddell, Peter. *The Thatcher Government*. Oxford and New York: Blackwell, 1985.

1790. Savoie, Donald J. *Thatcher, Reagan, Mulroney: In Search of a New Bureaucracy*. Pitt Series in Policy and Institutional Studies. Pittsburgh: University of Pittsburgh Press, 1994.

1791. Smith, Geoffrey. *Reagan and Thatcher*. 1st American ed. New York: W. W. Norton, 1991.

1792. Thatcher, Margaret. *The Downing Street Years*. New York: HarperCollins, 1993.

Famous People—Waldheim, Kurt (1918–)

1793. Bassett, Richard. *Waldheim and Austria*. New York: Penguin Books, 1989.

1794. Finger, Seymour Maxwell, and Arnold A. Saltzman. *Bending With the Winds: Kurt Waldheim and the United Nations*. New York: Praeger, 1990.

1795. Rosenbaum, Eli M., and William Hoffer. *Betrayal: The Untold Story of the Kurt Waldheim Investigation and Cover-Up*. New York: St. Martin's Press, 1993.

1796. Waldheim, Kurt. *In the Eye of the Storm: A Memoir*. Bethesda: Adler & Adler, 1986.

Famous People—Wilhelmina, Queen of the Netherlands (1880–1962)

1797. Jong, Louis de. *The Netherlands and Nazi Germany*. Cambridge: Harvard University Press, 1990.

Index

About the Author

Joan F. Higbee is a senior reference librarian in the Rare Book and Special Collections Division of the Library of Congress where she works with holdings that range from the largest collection of fifteenth century printed books in the Western Hemisphere to rare publications of the post World War II period. A member of the staff of the Library of Congress since 1976, she has served as a senior cataloger of contemporary Western European research publications and has written profiles of major research collections for the Library's European Division and its Motion Picture, Broadcasting and Recorded Sound Division.

Dr. Higbee is the author of *The Scholars' Guide to Washington, D.C. for Southwest European Studies* (Washington, D.C.: Wilson Center Press, 1989). She is a former chairperson of The Western European Specialists Section of the Association of College and Research Libraries and served for eight years on the policy-making Council of the American Library Association. Dr. Higbee received her M.A. and Ph.D. degrees in Romance Languages from The Johns Hopkins University (1975) and an M.S. in Library Science from The Catholic University of America (1976). She has studied at the Sorbonne, the Université de Nancy and the Collège International de Cannes. She has taught in both France and the United States and has published literary criticism in Europe and articles and reports germane to library science in France and the United States.